La Confiseuse.

Front endpapers: "The Chocolate Maid," painted in the nineteenth century by Liotard, has become a favorite motif in chocolate advertisements. An eighteenth-century French maiden is decked with a bounty of the fruit and nut morsels that grace filled chocolate confections.

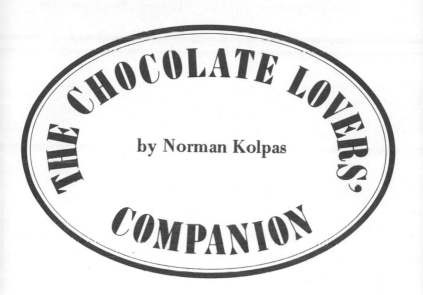

THE CHOCOLATE LOVERS' COMPANION

by Norman Kolpas

New York quick fox Tokyo

Contents

In Canada: Gage Trade Publishing, P.O. Box 5000, 164 Commander Blvd., Agincourt, Ontario M1S 3C7.

International Standard Book Number: 0-8256-3126-2
Library of Congress Catalog Card Number: 78-056219

Originally published in Holland in 1977

Cover design by Iris Weinstein
Cover photograph by Charles Fishbein

Chapter 1
Pre-Columbian Cocoa to Modern Chocolate Bar

Americain avec Sa Chocolatiere et Son Gobelet

Rameau de L'arbre du Cacao

cacao

Gousses de Vanille

An American native holds aloft a chocolate stirrer, while below him are shown cacao pods and the flavoring agent vanilla, in an engraving from a study of chocolate published in 1688 by the Frenchman Philippe Sylvestre Dufour.

History and Progress

Legend and Speculation

Anecdotes

The Food of the Gods

Around the middle of the eighteenth century, Carl von Linnaeus named the tree from which the raw material for cocoa and chocolate comes *Theobroma*, a pairing of Greek words to mean "Food of the Gods." None of the other multitudinous plants and animals classified by that pre-eminent Swedish naturalist received such an exalted appellation.

Throughout history mankind has, with few exceptions, exalted in the flavor, nutritive value and immense versatility of chocolate. Chocolate's history as beverage and food is in large part a story of how innovative people have sought to develop and improve it, bringing out the full potential of its natural goodness. This does not mean, however, that chocolate has had a peaceful history; at times it has been connected with moments of great human tragedy. And we shall also see that chocolate has sometimes even been disregarded altogether as a food, serving other surprising purposes instead.

This chapter highlights some key events and unusual aspects of the history of chocolate: food for thought the next time you nibble on a bar of the "Food of the Gods."

A Mythical Origin

As far back as the records left by early Latin American civilizations may be traced, the chocolate drink was a part of their daily lives. It must be left to obscure legend to give any explanation of how chocolate first came to be used.

12

Credit for this introduction is usually given to the feathered serpent god, known to the ancient Mexicans as Quetzalcoatl. This god of the air gave to his people the knowledge necessary for a higher existence; he taught them how to follow the paths of the stars, and provided them with a calendar; he showed them how to take the fluffy tufts of a wild plant, spin them into threads, and weave these threads into cotton cloth; they learned from him how to ornament themselves with jade and with cloaks made from feathers. Most important, he gave them maize and chocolate, staples previously enjoyed only by himself and the other gods in heaven.

The Toltec tribe, who lived in the area later occupied by the Aztecs, are said to have been ruled by Quetzalcoatl, who, unlike his subjects, was fair of face and bearded. One day, the great god-king was tricked by a rival god, Tezcatlipoca, into drinking a potion that reputedly could transport him to a faraway kingdom; instead, it robbed him of his divine courage and pride. The only thing for Quetzalcoatl to do was to leave his people. He destroyed and buried all his wealth, and changed his royal cacao trees into thorny mesquite shrubs. Then he traveled to the eastern coast of his kingdom, near the present-day site of Veracruz, and, boarding a raft made of serpents, he sailed away.

Before he left, Quetzalcoatl promised his people that, in the year of Ce Acatl, he would return from the direction in which he departed. We will see later how Quetzalcoatl's promise was sadly fulfilled by foreign invaders in 1519 (which corresponded to Ce Acatl in the Aztec calendar) when the Aztecs inhabited the lands of the Toltecs.

The earliest illustration of a cacao tree and its shade tree appeared in 1565 in Benzoni's History of the New World *(the copy below comes from the Dutch edition). The tree, fruit and distinctive blossom (above left) were scientifically classified some 200 years later by the Swedish botanist Linnaeus.*

Van den Boom die de Cacavate draegt, dat haer Geldt is, en hoe de Indianen uyt twee Houten Vyer krijgen.

13

Chocolate's Unremembered Inventor

Digressing from the Quetzalcoatl legend for a moment, it is interesting to speculate on how man first came to make use of the seeds of the cacao tree's fruit.

The German scientist and explorer von Humboldt, when he traveled through the Americas in the late eighteenth century, noted that the tribes he encountered along the Orinoco in Venezuela enjoyed sucking the sweet pulp of the cacao fruit, discarding the pod shell and the seeds. He saw no evidence that they brewed any sort of beverage from the seeds or the fruit.

At one time the Toltecs and other tribes that worshipped Quetzalcoatl merely savored the cacao fruit's pulp. And when they ventured to bite into a cacao seed, they were probably taken aback by its bitterness. Someone's disgust for the seeds must at some point have led him to throw them into the fire; and a few minutes later, when the fire gave forth a rich and pleasurable aroma, the thrower of the seeds must have traced the aroma to its source, and found that it came from the seeds themselves. Then tasting them anew, he discovered that fire transformed the worthless seeds into a delightful and valuable new food which, when ground and mixed with water and other ingredients, made an excellent beverage.

Mayan Religious Ritual and Chocolate

Chocolate was the gift of one of the most revered gods of the early Latin Americans. So it was only natural that the drink, and the cacao beans from which it is made, should have become an integral part of the religious rituals of these peoples.

The Mayans seem to have given great religious importance to chocolate. They believed in the continuation of a human spirit's life after bodily death. If the person had led a good, religious life, the spirit could hope to dwell in the benevolent shade of the first tree in the world. And the perpetual refreshment served beneath this tree was chocolate.

In his study of *The Native Races of the Pacific States of North America*, Hubert Howe Bancroft detailed some chocolate rituals, including sacrifices:

''In the month of Muan the cacao-planters held a festival in honor of the gods Ekchuah, Chac, and Hobnil, who were their patron deities. To solemnize it, they all went to the

An illustration from a history of Latin America published around 1500 portrays the ceremonial dignity surrounding the sale of a cup of chocolate at a public stall.

plantation of one of their number, where they sacrificed a dog having a spot on its skin the color of cacao. They burned incense to their idols, and made offerings of blue iguanas, feathers of a particular kind of bird, and game. After this they gave to each of the officials a branch of the cacao-plant. The sacrifice being ended, they all sat down to a repast, at which, it is said, no one was allowed to drink more than three glasses of wine. All then went into the house of him who had given the feast, and passed the time pleasantly together."

Commerce and Chocolate

In civilizations that were so totally dominated by religion and its rituals, it is no wonder that chocolate—as the gift of a god—should have become so highly valued that it was more than just a food. Chocolate was, first of all, a drink enjoyed largely by the wealthier classes of the advanced Latin American tribes. Beyond that, its value made it a popular form of currency. (In fact, there was even a valuable metallic compound, used by a tribe in southern Mexico, that was given the name "cacao.")

Hubert Howe Bancroft detailed the currency system of the Nahuas, a Mexican tribe, based on nibs or grains of a particular species of cacao:

"This money, known as *patlachté*, passed current anywhere, and payments of it were made by count up to eight thousand, which constituted a *xiquipilli*. In large transactions sacks containing three xiquipilli were used to save labor in counting."

Accounts of chocolate currency such as this caused at least one European historian to declare it "blessed money which exempts its possessors from avarice, since it cannot be hoarded nor hidden underground." But some of the uses to which this money was put could hardly be called blessed.

Huge quantities of cacao beans were a regular part of the tributes paid by small tribes to larger, conquering ones. In 1725 Sir Hans Sloane noted an instance of this, and supplied an equivalent value in silver (Real of Plate): "The Indians of the desolate province of Soconusco pay the King their tribute in Cacao, giving him 400 cargas, and every carga is 24,000 almonds [cacao beans], which is worth 30 pieces of Real of Plate."

Another form of misery for which chocolate was common currency was slavery. Note the market rates, as recorded by Bancroft, for the two following commodities: " . . . a rabbit in Nicaragua sold for ten cacao-nibs, and one hundred of these seeds would buy a tolerably good slave." The Mayans were great dealers in slaves from conquered tribes, and wherever they were sold one hundred beans was the going price. (You could get a pumpkin for only four cacao beans, so in terms of bartering you might say that a slave was also worth twenty-five pumpkins.)

If the need to buy a human body was for a more transitory purpose, the price was better. The services of certain Mayan women could be had for a mere eight to ten cacao beans a night.

Tributes of chocolate paid by Mexican tribes to their king were recorded in hieroglyphs representing basketloads of different sizes.

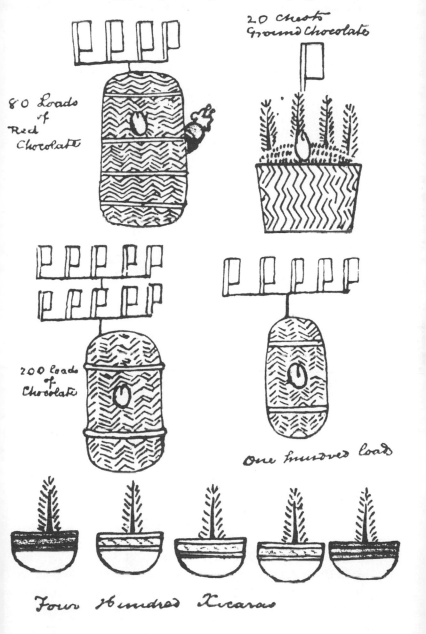

The great Aztec emperor Montezuma was also history's greatest chocolate drinker: he consumed some 50 pitchers full each day.

In the Halls of Montezuma

The first European to encounter chocolate, it is said, was Columbus. On his fourth voyage in search of a trade route to India, he arrived in Nicaragua on July 30, 1502. He saw the natives using chocolate as a drink and for trade; but it made absolutely no impact on him. He sailed on, leaving chocolate where it was.

In 1519, the year known to the Aztecs as Ce Acatl, another Spanish ship arrived in Latin America, on the eastern shore of Mexico. The Spanish party was led by Hernando Cortez. He was, naturally, light-skinned, and in the fashion of the day sported a beard. The Aztecs thought their god Quetzalcoatl had returned.

Cortez and his men were welcomed into the resplendent palace of the Aztec emperor, Montezuma. And there they were treated to one of the most luxurious of his enjoyments—the service of chocolate. The historian Prescott described the elaborate way in which Montezuma daily took the beverage:

"The emperor took no other beverage than the Chocolatl, a potation of Chocolate flavoured with vanilla and other spices, and so prepared as to be reduced to a froth of the consistency of honey, which gradually dissolved in the mouth, and was taken cold. This beverage, if so it could be called, was served in golden goblets, with spoons of the same metal, or of tortoiseshell finely wrought. The emperor was exceedingly fond of it, to judge from the quantity—no less than fifty jars or pitchers being prepared for his own daily consumption: two thousand more were allowed for that of his household."

The Spanish had never seen anything quite like Montezuma's chocolate drink, let alone the splendor in which it was served. In fact, the obvious monetary value of chocolate impressed them far more than the cold, thick, bitter and peppery preparation the Aztecs concocted. Cortez ordered that a Spanish cacao plantation be set up to raise the remarkably barterable crop. And attracted by all the other wealth he saw in the possession of the emperor, he set about cruelly to conquer the Aztec kingdom. In 1528 Cortez carried the first cacao beans home to Spain, as part of his plunder taken from the people of the god Quetzalcoatl.

A Spicy, Scummy Drink

An idea of the sort of chocolate encountered by the Spaniards may be had from the Englishman Thomas Gage, who traveled to Latin America in the early seventeenth century and related his adventures in 1648 in a book entitled *A New Survey of the West Indies*. In a chapter devoted largely to chocolate, he details the ingredients and actions that went into the preparation of the beverage as drunk by the common people:

"The *Cacao*, and the other ingredients must be beaten in a mortar of stone, or (as the *Indians* use) ground upon a broad stone, which they call *Metate*, and is only made for that use. But first the ingredients are all to be dried, except the

19

Achiotte [a red coloring agent], with care that they may be beaten to powder, keeping them still in stirring, that they be not burnt or become black; for if they be over-dried, they will be bitter and lose their Virtue. The Cinnamon and the long red Pepper are to be first beaten with the Anniseed, and then the *Cacao*, which must be beaten by little and little, till it be all powdred; and in the beating it must be turn'd round, that it may mix the better. Every one of these ingredients must be beaten by it self, and then all be put into the Vessel, where the *Cacao* is, which you must stir together with a Spoon, and then take out that Paste, and put it into the mortar, under which there must be a little Fire, after the confection is made, but if more Fire be put under than will only warm it, the unctuous part will dry away. The *Achiotte* also must be put in in the beating, that it may the better take the colour. When it is well beaten and incorporated (which will be known by the shortness of it) then with a Spoon is taken up some of the paste, which will be almost liquid, and made into Tablets, or else without a Spoon put into Boxes, and when it is cold it will be hard. Those that make it into Tablets, put a spoon full of the paste upon a piece of Paper (the *Indians* put it upon the leaf of a plantin Tree) where being put into the shade (for in the Sun it melts and

A present-day Mexican shop assistant weighs roasted cacao beans – a commodity that has played an important role in her country for centuries.

Aztec women roast and grind cacao, in a sixteenth-century engraving (above) from the work of Benzoni. Once ground the cacao was mixed with water using a stirrer, or molinet *(below).*

dissolves) it grows hard; and then bowing the paper or leaf the Tablet falls off, by reason of the fatness of the paste. But if it be put into anything of earth, or Wood, it sticks fast, and will not come off, but with scraping or breaking. The manner of drinking it, is divers; the one (being the way most us'd in *Mexico*) is to take it hot with Atolle [a cornmeal gruel drink], dissolving a Tablet in hot Water, and then stirring and beating it in the Cup where it is to be drunk, with a Molinet [a wooden stick carved especially for mixing chocolate], and when it is well stirr'd to a scum or froth, then to fill the cup with hot Atolle, and so drink it sup by sup.''

European settlers almost immediately began to experiment with the concoction of chocolate. Nutmegs, cloves, different sorts of peppers, ambergris and lemon peel were mixed with the drink. But the most prevalent, and lasting, additions were three: ground almonds and other nuts, forerunners of the whole roasted nuts that bring such variety to modern chocolate bars; vanilla beans, native to Mexico, which smoothed and sweetened the rough flavor of the chocolate drink, and are today the most common flavoring of chocolate; and most important, sugar, which made and still makes chocolate a joy to the most delicate of palates.

Murder by Chocolate

Chocolate was certainly involved, from time to time, in what civilized men consider barbaric and cruel practices. One remarkable episode, related by Thomas Gage, shows that early European settlers in Latin America were capable of killing not only the natives, but also each other for, and with the help of, their chocolate.

The ladies of Chiapa, a city near Mexico's border with Guatemala, found that they were "not able to continue in the Church while the Mass is hudl'd over, much less while a solemn high Mass (as they call it) is sung, and a Sermon preach'd, unless they drink a Cup of hot Chocolatte, and eat a bit of sweet-meats to strengthen their Stomachs. For this purpose they were wont to make their Maids bring them to Church in the middle of Mass or Sermon a cup of Chocolatte, which could not be done to all, or most of them without great Confusion, and interrupting both Mass and Sermon."

These gentle women were warned against this practice by the bishop of Chiapa. But the following Sunday, the chocolate commotion in church was as great as usual. The bishop had no choice, then, but to "fix in Writing on the Church Doors an excommunication against all such as should presume at the time of Service to eat or drink in the Church."

Even this stern action did not have the desired effect. The women of Chiapa, Gage tells us, did take the bishop's threat to heart; it grieved them to think that, for the sake of their chocolate, they would have to give up going to church. A leading lady of the community approached Gage and a friendly prior, asking them to see if they could persuade the bishop to alter his firm position:

"The good Prior and my self Labour'd all we could, alledging the Custom of the Country, the weakness of the Sex whom it most concern'd, also the weakness of their Stomachs, the Contempt that might thence ensue to his Person, and many Inconveniences which might follow to the breeding of an uproar in the Church and City, whereof we had some probable Conjecture from what already we had heard. But none of these Reasons would move the Bishop, to which he answer'd that he preferr'd the honour of God, and of his House before his own Life."

Prophetic words.

Seeing the bishop unmoved, most of the women resolved to flout his authority. They showed up in church and, ignoring all threats of excommunication, drank their chocolate "as the Fish doth Water." The bishop ordered his priests to take the chocolate forcibly from the maids as they delivered it to their mistresses. Husbands and suitors drew their swords against the men of the church.

After this incident, most of the citizens of Chiapa stayed away from the city's cathedral, going instead to nearby cloisters "where by the Nuns and Friers they were not troubl'd." In fact, the holy people of these cloisters were "talked of far and near, not for their religious practices," but for their skill in making chocolate. Devout families who used to give generous donations to the cathedral, now bestowed their money on these unusually talented nuns and friars.

This enraged the bishop even more, and he began threatening excommunication left and right, for the clergy as well as the laity. For a month the women simply stayed at home; and during that time, entirely unexpectedly, the bishop fell terribly ill. He was brought to a Dominican cloister (not one of the chocolate-making ones) for care.

"Physicians were sent for far and near," Gage tells us, "who all with a joynt Opinion agreed that the Bishop was

A refined young woman of high social rank takes her chocolate with an innocent air, in a nineteenth-century French lithograph.

LE GOÛT.

poysn'd, and he himself doubt'd not of it at his death praying God to forgive those that had been the Cause of it . . . ."

Gage followed up the bishop's death with some personal detective work, much as a modern investigative reporter would pursue a story:

"A Gentile Woman with whom I was well acquainted in that City, who was noted to be somewhat too Familiar with one of the Bishops Pages, was commonly censur'd to have prescribed such a Cup of Chocolat to be ministred by the Page, which poison'd him who so rigorously had forbidden Chocolat to be drunk in the Church. My self heard this Gentlewoman say of the deceased Bishop, that she thought few griev'd for his Death, and that the Women had no reason to grieve for him, and that she judg'd, he being such an Enemy to Chocolat in the Church, that which he had drunk at home had not agreed with his body. . . . The Women of this City are somewhat light in their Carriage, and have learn'd from the Devil many enticing Lessons and Baits to draw poor Souls to Sin and Damnation; and if they cannot have their Wills, they surely Work Revenge by Chocolat. . . ."

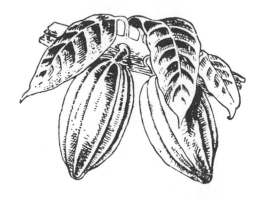

Spanish Monopoly—Dutch and English Scorn

Thomas Gage wrote about chocolate well over a hundred years after tablets of the prepared cacao bean and brewing equipment were first carried to Spain. His detailed description of the beverage, the beans and the tree from which they came was made possible only because Spain was beginning its decline as a world power. For more than a century, the Spanish had managed to monopolize the cultivation and preparation of chocolate, keeping the delicacy safely ensconced south of the Pyrenees.

Of course other nations did have the occasional brush with chocolate. But unlike the Spaniards, they had no idea how palatable the drink could be made. Dutch and English pirates, for instance, found captured cargoes of cacao worse than worthless, as Gage humorously related in a passage on the scarcity of cacao in England:

"But how then might this Cacao with the other *Indian* ingredients be had in *England*? even by trading in *Spain* for it, as we do for other Commodities; or not sleighting it so much as we and the *Hollanders* have often done upon the *Indian* seas; of whom I have heard the *Spaniards* say that when we have taken a good prize, a ship laden with *Cacao*, in anger and wrath we have hurl'd over board this good Commodity, not regarding the worth and goodness of it, but calling it in bad *Spain, Cagaruta de Carnero*, or Sheeps Dung in good *English*. It was one of the necessariest commodities in the *India's*, and nothing enriches *Chiapa* in particular more than it, whither are brought from *Mexico* and other parts, the Rich Bags of Patacons, only for the *Cagaruta de Carnero*, which we call Sheeps Dung."

An engraving from a seventeenth-century Latin book shows a native presenting Neptune with chocolate to carry across the seas.

Taking Up Chocolate for Lent

Chocolate's first giant step north of the Pyrenees came in 1615, with the marriage of Anne of Austria, daughter of King Phillip III of Spain, to King Louis XIII of France. The beverage quickly became the vogue of the French court; and the fashion was given even greater support with another royal link, when the Spanish princess Maria Theresa married King Louis XIV in 1660.

Even more important to the spread of chocolate, however, were the Spanish monks who carried the sustaining beverage to their meditative brethren in other countries. Granted, a few men of religion did not take kindly to the drink; for example, in 1624 in Vienna, Joan Franc Rauch published his *"Disputatio medico diœtetica de aëre et esculentis, de necnon potû,"* which criticized many of those who took holy orders as having violated their most sacred vows. He placed much of the blame on chocolate as an inflamer of passions, suggested that it be forbidden to monks, and concluded "that if such an interdiction had existed that scandal with which that holy order had been branded might have proved groundless."

But chocolate was due for approbation from higher echelons. At first the approval was of a backhanded sort: Pope Pius V tasted chocolate in 1569; he found the drink so disgusting that he was sure no one would ever make a habit of it, and so he could safely rule that it did not constitute a break of fast. And in 1662 more positive acceptance of the drink came from Cardinal Brancaccio, who ruled that liquids, such as chocolate, did not break the fast (*"Liquidum non frangit jejunum"*).

In 1748 the Italian theological scholar Daniel Concuna published a treatise which summarized all the wars of words that had been waged over chocolate and fasting. It was, he pointed out, a real trial of conscience:

"Consumers are, without the help of casuists, troubled themselves and afflicted when in Lent they empty Chocolate cups. Excited on the one hand by the pungent cravings of the throat to moisten it, reproved on the other by breaking their fast, they experience grave remorse of conscience, and, with consciences agitated and torn with drinking the sweet beverage, they sin."

And Concuna highlighted, with tongue in cheek, the practical creativity of religion as demonstrated by Father Tommaso Hurtado, who devoted the entire tenth treatise of the second volume (plus an appendix) of his *Moral Resolutions*, published in 1651, to the justification of taking chocolate during the Lentin fast:

"For all agree," Concuna summed up, "that he will break his fast who eats any portion of chocolate, which, dissolved and well mixed with warm water, is not prejudicial to keeping a fast. This is a sufficiently marvellous presupposition. He who eats four ounces of exquisite sturgeon roasted has broken his fast; if he has it dissolved and prepared in an extract of thick broth, he does not sin."

A Very Good Cup of "Jocolatte"

Gradually winning over all who tasted it in its ever-improving forms, chocolate slowly gained acceptance throughout Europe. At times, of course, it did have difficulties, but these were not necessarily caused by its flavor or any ill effects ascribed to it. Instead, as a desirable commodity, it was met with trade restrictions by insular European countries. In Prussia, for example, the first half of the eighteenth century saw chocolate first slapped with heavy import duties by Frederick I (1704), and later forbidden by Frederick the Great from being hawked in public (1747). But chocolate nevertheless continued to rise in popularity, to such a degree that the great dramatist Goethe, as one of countless devotees of the beverage, would pack chocolate and a chocolate pot in his luggage whenever he traveled, to be certain of always getting a perfect cup of his favorite drink.

An elegant German couple are served with the popular new drink chocolate, in an early eighteenth-century engraving.

Cocoa is consumed with lively enjoyment in a seventeenth-century English chocolate house.

Chocolate also met with some government opposition through import duties in England, where the first chocolate house was opened in London by a French chocolateer in 1657. Coffeehouses had opened in the city some five years earlier; but already they were so much frequented by the general populace that the upper crust had need of a gentler, more refined setting for their socializing. The chocolate house, because of the heavily taxed, high cost of the beverage (ten to fifteen shillings for a pound of the raw material alone), perfectly suited aristocratic needs. And it was not just the social aristocracy that found the chocolate houses to their liking; on November 24, 1664, the diarist Samuel Pepys recorded that he had been, "To a coffee house to drink jocolatte, very good."

In a book on chocolate the Austrian writer Silbermann briefly chronicled the advance of the English chocolate house:

"After the Restoration there were shops in London for the sale of Chocolate at ten shillings or fifteen shillings per pound. Ozinda's chocolate house was full of aristocratic customers. Comedies, satirical essays, the memoirs and private letters of that age frequently mention it. The habit of using chocolate was deemed a token of elegant and fashionable taste, and . . . the learned physicians extolled its medicinal virtues."

The Dutch Develop Delightful Cocoa

Well into the nineteenth century, chocolate remained a drink that bore little similarity to the beverage or the food we enjoy today, in spite of any improvements made in its flavor. Thick, grainy, sugared cakes of chocolate became, when mixed with hot water, a beverage that was thick and very rich with the fat of the roasted cacao beans. Even when farinaceous substances, such as the Mexican's cornmeal, were added to counteract the fat, the drink was still relatively difficult to digest. In 1828, however, the manufacture of chocolate finally took a great leap forward, in Holland.

C. J. van Houten owned and operated a chocolate factory in the town of Weesp. He was one of many chocolate makers in Holland, where the drink had been very popular since about 1660 (Dutch chocolate houses carried the signs *"Hier schenkt men Socculate"*—"Here chocolate is served"). Van Houten was a competitive man, and a proud one, and he wanted his chocolate to be finer than any of the others produced by his countrymen.

He was especially concerned with the digestibility of his chocolate. He knew that the high fat content of the product made the drink far too rich for delicate appetites; but he did

Workers power a chocolate grinding mill, in an early scene from the van Houten factory on the Leliegracht in Amsterdam.

not believe in adulterating the drink with cornmeal or other flours that merely disguised the fat and made the drink thicker and less pure. The best that could normally be done then was to spoon off what little fat separated from the drink and floated on the surface of the chocolate cup. But, van Houten reasoned, if some of the fat content separates out by itself, why not see if more can be made to do so mechanically?

To this end, van Houten invented the first primitive cocoa press, that squeezed and filtered freshly ground cacao beans to extract a flow of liquid cocoa butter and leave a dry, low-fat cake of hard cocoa (more about the technical side of this process in the next chapter). And van Houten went further in his refinement of the cocoa drink by inventing the alkalizing process now known as "Dutching," which makes cocoa powder even more digestible by neutralizing its natural acid content, while making it mix more smoothly and evenly with liquids (more about this in the next chapter as well).

North American Newcomers to Chocolate

It is possible that the Dutch were the first to introduce chocolate to North America. They no doubt carried the popular new drink in cargo ships from Amsterdam to New Amsterdam some time before they lost their colony in 1664.

But chocolate really got a strong foothold in America some hundred years later, as one of the commodities carried by Yankee traders from the West Indies back to New England. And the first impetus for the manufacture of chocolate in the American colonies naturally came from Europe, with the arrival in Boston in 1765 of John Hannon, an experienced chocolate maker from Great Britain. With the financial assistance of Dr. James Baker, a resident of the Massachusetts Bay Colony, Hannon set up a factory in a deserted grist mill on the Neponset River near the town of Dorchester. Soon he was advertising his wares with a confidence and integrity that was peculiarly, brashly American:

Hannon's Best CHOCOLATE Marked upon each Cake J.H.N. Warranted pure, & ground exceeding fine. Where may be had any Quantity, from 50 wt. to a ton, for Cash or Cocoa, at his Mills in Milton.
N.B. If the Chocolate does not
prove good, the Money will
be returned.

In 1900 this electric automobile was a wise piece of publicity for the new Hershey factory in Pennsylvania. The first to be seen there, it represented the company's innovative modernity.

Twelve years after starting the business, Hannon disappeared while on a business trip, and never returned. The silent partner Dr. Baker took over, and the business thrived under him and has been passed down through the Baker family to this day.

Americans rapidly took to chocolate, and its manufacture and consumption was not limited to its original colonial roots. In the middle of the nineteenth century, for example, a small chocolate factory was set up in the wild Gold Rush town of San Francisco by an Italian immigrant who arrived there by way of South America and the chocolate-rich countries of Central America. Domingo Ghirardelli's business gained in popularity; and today his old chocolate manufactory has been renovated and forms the core of an immensely popular tourist attraction—Ghirardelli Square.

At times, Americans needed some help in order to learn to love chocolate. In 1878, for example, a chocolate manufacturer named Henry Maillard actually set up a free "chocolate school" to help potential customers learn the correct way to use his products. A wise businessman.

Of course no one has heard of Henry Maillard's chocolate for many years. But the wisest chocolate businessman of all was so successful that his name became synonymous with the chocolate bar: Milton Snavely Hershey.

After carefully studying the chocolate market in the United States, the forty-three-year-old Hershey started a chocolate factory in 1900, near his birthplace in Derry Church, Pennsylvania. Production in his extremely modern factory began in December of the following year; and within ten years his sales had reached a level of some $5 million.

Hershey began by producing just two main products, the regular milk chocolate Hersheybar and the Hersheybar With Almonds. For the milk in his chocolate he relied on the dairy lands surrounding his factory. But his success in fact depended more importantly—as has that of all twentieth century manufacturers—on some developments in Switzerland just a few years earlier.

Pioneers of Swiss Chocolate

Nestlé, Lindt, Peter, Tobler, Suchard: all names that conjure up mouthwatering images of a wide range of delicious chocolates. But how many of us are aware of the fact that these are also the names of men who, in the nineteenth century, revolutionized the making—and eating—of chocolate and brought worldwide fame to the confectionary products of their native Switzerland?

The Swiss first became acquainted with chocolate toward the end of the seventeenth century, as travelers to Belgium, France, England and especially Italy brought back glowing reports of the delicious drink. Soon after 1720 a steady

Elaborate chocolate creations were displayed in the first Suchard shop (below) in Serrières. The company also caught the public eye with souvenir cards (right) depicting the many times of day at which their cocoa could be enjoyed.

8 Heures
DÉJEUNER.

9 Heures — LECTURE.

stream of Italian chocolate makers enjoyed fruitful visits to Switzerland. The Swiss themselves began to prove that they were reputable chocolateers in 1792, when two brothers opened a highly successful chocolate shop and factory in Berlin; the locals actually appraised their chocolate as being "first rate."

Finally, in 1819, François-Louis Cailler opened the first chocolate factory in Switzerland on the northeastern shore of Lake Geneva in a deserted mill near Vevey. Cailler was a true devotee of chocolate; he first tasted it at a local fair where it was made by Italian hawkers, and he was so impressed that he emigrated to Italy to spend four years learning the trade first hand as a factory apprentice.

A few years later, Alexis Suchard followed Cailler's example, opening in Serrières a factory which reached an output of as much as seventy pounds of chocolate a day. And the only factory workers were Suchard and his one assistant.

Other chocolate factories soon sprang up throughout Switzerland. But the first real step towards Swiss innovation began not in the confectionary industry but in that of breakfast cereals, when Henri Nestlé developed a process for making condensed milk for the production of children's groats.

33

This laid some of the groundwork for the inventive Daniel Peter of Vevey. While a young candlemaker Peter had met and fallen in love with Fanny Cailler, the eldest daughter of the pioneer Swiss chocolate maker. Peter was soon following a new occupation. In 1875, with the aid of Nestle's condensed milk, he developed a method for producing a solid combination of chocolate and milk: the first solid milk chocolate.

There is no doubt that Peter's invention alone changed the world chocolate industry for ever. But no one did more for the industry than yet another great Swiss confectioner, Rodolphe Lindt, who operated a chocolate factory below Berne cathedral in the latter part of the nineteenth century.

An elegant skater spelled out the name of the chocolate to buy in an advertisement for the maker of the first milk chocolate.

Fabrique de Chocolats Rod. Lindt Fils à Berne (Suisse)

The spire of Berne cathedral can be seen beyond the chocolate factory of Rodolphe Lindt (above). Lindt made the world's first fondant chocolate (below), carefully processed for several days.

Lindt brought the true spirit of invention to the manufacture of chocolate. He was always tinkering with his basic equipment, forever altering ingredients, doggedly trying different methods and timings in his small factory. One week, he decided to process a batch of chocolate over a period of several days, continually mixing it in a long, narrow trough. He was amazed by the result: a chocolate without a hint of the grainy texture previously present in even the most carefully refined solid products. Realizing he had happened on something that would make his chocolate better than anyone else's, Lindt still did not rest on his laurels; instead, he experimented by adding extra cocoa butter to the chocolate while it was undergoing this new process; this gave it even more smoothness and unsurpassed melting qualities. Rodolphe Lindt had invented the process now known as conching, and with it fondant chocolate. Almost every chocolate bar you consume today is a direct result of this one man's work.

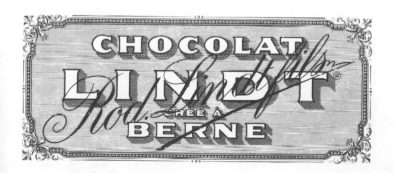

Botany and Agriculture

History

Commerce and Industry

Amusements

On the Gold Coast in Ghana a plantation worker stolidly bears the weight of a bag of cacao beans en route to the docks from which they will be shipped to foreign markets.

You Say Cacao and I Say Cocoa

Every time you ask for a cup of "cocoa," you are making a mistake, although you do have a very good excuse for making it: the error has been handed down to you over two centuries of usage.

When, at the beginning of the sixteenth century, Spanish explorers were first introduced to cocoa in the court of the Aztec emperor Montezuma, they imitated the sound of the native word for the drink and came up with *cacao*. This word was carried back to Europe with the beans and the beverage, and it spread into common usage—except in England, where speech characteristics could not twist themselves easily around such a stick-in-the-throat word. Cacao was corrupted into cocoa, and it has stayed that way ever since.

Meanwhile, the Swedish botanist Linnaeus classified the source of cacao as *Theobroma cacao*, from the Greek words $\theta\varepsilon\delta\varsigma$ (Gods) and $\beta\rho\hat{\omega}\mu\alpha$ (food), thus dubbing the tree and its fruit, "Cacao: Food of the Gods."

So here, the word "cacao" is used with reference to the raw product—the tree and its pods and beans. Only when processed do they become what we know as "cocoa."

A Tropical Fantasy: The Cacao Tree

A favorite gimmick of fashionably expensive restaurants and nightclubs is to create a tropical fantasy environment: palm trees and other exotic foliage (usually plastic) sway in the breeze from the ventilation shaft while artificial stars twinkle above, waitresses in scant grass skirts serve long, fruity drinks, and a musical combo plays music with an infectious beat.

The cacao tree would not look out of place in such a den of tropical hokum. It looks as though it was created by a half-crazed interior designer who was given full creative rein.

It is a tall, slender tree, that may reach as high as sixty feet in the wild, but is usually no higher than twenty-five feet when cultivated. Most of its fragile branches are not much thicker than the trunk. The tree's foliage is evergreen, but before the leaves reach their large, glossy green maturity they usually turn red.

The tree's trunk is often decked with mosses and lichens, colorful and mostly harmless parasites that thrive in the tropical shade and humidity. In addition, tiny orchids may cling to the branches, adding delicate, pure pastel decorations.

In addition, the cacao has its own little blossoms, clusters of five-petaled waxy white or pink flowers. These blossoms

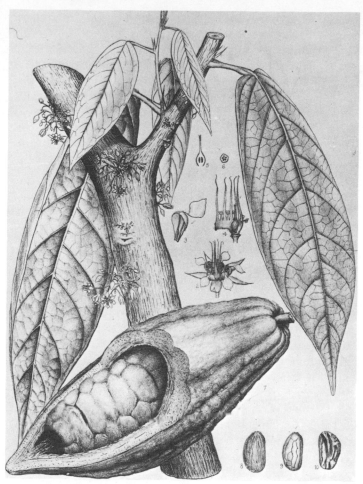

An English botanical drawing shows in detail the cacao tree, including: its trunk and a branch with leaves and blossom (1); its blossom (2–6); a pod and the beans within (7); and the bean's structure (8–10). Cacao is wisely labeled a "medicinal plant."

do not, however, behave in the usual way. Instead of appearing along the boughs of the tree, they huddle directly on the trunk and the strong, main branches. And the trees blossom continuously and abundantly, producing as many as a hundred thousand flowers in a year.

Only a fraction of these flowers are lucky enough to develop into fruit, or cacao pods; at most about thirty pods a year grow on any one tree. As the tree flowers year-round, pods can be seen in various stages of development along with fresh blossoms all the time.

The pods, as they mature, look even more incongruous than the blossoms did. They are green when small; but as they grow to a maximum size of ten inches and a diameter of three to four, the rough-textured shell of the pod progresses

39

through yellow to a russet brown. And no tree-grown fruit could look stranger than they do, hanging all along the trunk from stems no longer than an inch. It looks as if someone had come across the tree and decided it would look better if it were covered with a jumble of gay lanterns. Sometimes one of these pods bursts out of the earth beside the tree, an exuberant outgrowth of the root.

Of course, the most remarkable thing about the cacao tree is what is inside the pods. But before we actually split one open, we should have a look at the care man must give to cultivating *Theobroma cacao*.

A Nonconformist Tree

Strange as it may seem, very few cacao plantations in the Western hemisphere are composed of trees belonging exclusively to one subspecies of cacao tree. Not that it cannot be: some more modern plantations, such as those in West Africa, have been started from the cuttings of single mother trees. But the cacao tree cross-pollinates very freely, trading genetic characteristics with its neighbors as readily as some people trade gossip. In effect, no single cacao tree possesses a complete set of features that can accurately distinguish it as belonging to a specific type of cacao.

Still, there are two basic, and very broad, groups into which cacao may be divided, along with a third (and according to some botanists and growers even a fourth) group as a sort of catchall for nonconformists.

The finest and rarest of cacao trees, making up only ten percent of world production, is *Criollo*—a name derived from the Spanish word for Creole, or native. These trees, indigenous to Central and South America, produce what is sometimes referred to as "the prince of cacaos." Their pods are long, slender and bumpy (in Mexico, *Criollo* is sometimes called "alligator" cacao). The cacao beans themselves are light in color, have soft skins, and give off a pleasant aroma; they result in a chocolate so exquisite that they are used only for products of the very highest quality, or to add a special touch to the taste of blended chocolates. As befits its rare and delicate flavor, *Criollo* is a very delicate tree; it is highly susceptible to disease, gives a relatively low crop yield, and ripens later than other cacaos.

The real workhorse of the cacaos is *Forastero*. Its name derives from the Spanish for outsider or foreigner; although it too is native to Latin America, compared to *Criollo* it is a relative newcomer to cultivation. Nevertheless, *Forastero*

The slender trunk and branches of a fully grown plantation tree are heavily laden with a rich crop of cacao pods.

and related subgroups account for about nine-tenths of the world's cacao crops. The trees have a high and hearty yield. But their plump, purple beans generally have a much harsher flavor than their *Criollo* cousins.

Hybrids on a middle ground between the two basic groups are sometimes lumped together as *Trinitario*. Their qualities range anywhere along the scale of characteristics from *Criollo* to *Forastero*, and they are often found simply grouped with one or the other. Although these hybrids occur naturally, there are others that are being scientifically created. It is hoped that, some day in the near future, a cacao hybrid will be created that will perfectly combine the robustness of *Forastero* with the delicacy of *Criollo*.

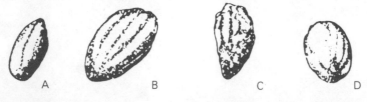

Black Pod, Witches' Broom and Other Horrors

Cacao trees have their enemies. They are prey to a great variety of insects and parasites that endanger their pod productions and their lives. And as fantastical as the trees themselves may appear, so their enemies sometimes seem to be as creepily malevolent as the evil beasties that stalk some bedtime stories.

The most widespread of these diseases, known as black pod, is caused by a fungal parasite called *Phytophthora palmivora*. It is a pervasive enemy, its spores capable of being carried on the air, by water, and on animals ranging from snails to small squirrels.

The first sign of black pod is the appearance of a small, dark brown or black spot on the pod. This spot enlarges, keeping roughly circular in shape, until it covers the entire pod. Rotting usually spreads inward as well, affecting the beans of young pods. The disease spreads rapidly, blackening neighboring pods and leaves. It has been estimated that some ten percent of world cacao production has been lost in this way.

Another visually bizarre and economically disastrous enemy of cacao is *Crinipellis perniciosa*, more commonly known as witches' broom. This disease has, over the past hundred years, severely damaged crops in Surinam, Guyana (where it entirely stopped exports from 1923 to 1930), Ecuador, Trinidad (where some infected plantations became research stations for investigating the disease) and elsewhere.

The flavor qualities of the four different types of cacao shown above left are as distinctive as their appearance: Angoleta (A); Red Amelonado (B); Calabacillo (C); Criollo (D). All varieties require protection from disease, and are regularly sprayed (above).

43

The fungus, when it infects a bud on the cacao tree, causes it to grow as a densely clustered bunch of shoots, which does in fact bear a remarkable resemblance to a witch's broom. The spores infect the pods as well, causing them to grow in stunted or distorted shapes and to rot.

Still other enemies attack cacao. Tiny brown bugs called capsids, especially prevalent in West Africa, eat the pods, shoots and branches of the tree. And a virus causing a condition known as swollen shoot means almost certain death within two years of the first sign of its symptoms.

Time and experience, and disaster, have taught cacao farmers to take special care in preventing crop disease. A great deal of money is spent on developing disease-resistant hybrids. Crops are sprayed regularly with fungicides and insecticides. And in severe cases such as swollen shoot, trees must be swiftly destroyed before disease can spread. The greater the control that can be exercised by the planter, the surer he can be of an abundant crop.

The Cacao Climate

Cacao trees thrive on heat and moisture. Their ideal average temperature is around 80° F; and depending on the drainage conditions of the rich soil they grow in, they need between

The dots on the map below show the distribution of cacao culture throughout the world's tropical regions. Vanilla (right), a plant which grows under the same conditions, is used to flavor many chocolates and cocoas.

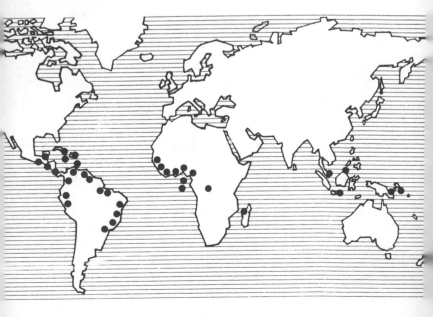

fifty and two hundred inches of rainfall each year, spread fairly evenly throughout the year rather than concentrated in any one season.

These conditions can be found in the tropics, within a zone fifteen to twenty degrees north and south of the equator. Cacao is, of course, native to such a climate, having first grown wild in the rainforests of what is now the Amazon basin (as Brazilians tell the story), or the Orinoco valley (as Venezuelans like to think) or the Chiapa district (as Mexicans believe). In any case, it is certain that as early as the seventh century the Mayas had established cacao plantations in the Yucatan peninsula. Cacao cultivation spread through Mexico and Central America: the Aztecs were practitioners of the art of *cacahuaquahuitl*, or cacao growing. But organized plantations did not really become the rule further south until the coming of Jesuit missionaries, who helped the natives tame wild cacao.

In 1525, cacao started to move abroad, when Spanish merchants began cultivation in Trinidad. Cacao soon spread throughout the Antilles. Within a century, cacao was being grown in the Caribbean. Then it was carried to the Philippines, to coastal islands off Africa and, by the Dutch, to Java and Sumatra.

Cacao culture began in Africa in the late 1870s, after a Gold Coast blacksmith saw the thriving plantations on the island of Fernando Po and carried a pod from there back to his home. This pod gave rise to the cacao plantations of Ghana, now the world's leading producer of the beans.

Today cacao is grown throughout Central and the northern part of South America, along the Atlantic coastal countries of central Africa, and on the islands of southeast Asia. For many of these countries, especially the developing African nations, cacao farming has grown to the point of becoming a major source of export revenue and, because of this, a major force for economic and social progress.

Two Brazilians reach their wild cacao trees by dugout canoe, in this nineteenth-century engraving.

Creating a Cacao Plantation

When a planter wants to begin cultivating cacao, he usually, and logically, chooses for his site a place where the cacao tree grows, or could grow, naturally. He goes to the edge of the tropical forest, where there is already natural shelter, warm humidity, and the rich soil that can only come from an abundance of constantly growing, dying and decaying plant matter.

First the undergrowth of the forest floor has to be cleared away. Next, the planter has to cut down trees to make room for his cacao. But he will not destroy all of the trees; a line of them will be left for about fifty to a hundred feet on either side, to serve as a windbreak to shelter the delicate cacao trees. And other, even more important trees will be left.

These are select shade trees near which the cacao will be planted. Cacao so badly requires protection from direct sunlight that the trees that "stand guard" over them are commonly referred to as "*Madres de cacao*," or "Cacao mothers." Where suitable trees do not exist to do this babysitting especially good shade trees will be planted: baobabs, lemons, bananas, coconuts and other large, hearty and leafy growths.

Of greatest importance to the plantation, of course, are the cacao trees themselves. The planter will carefully select seeds from the strongest, most disease-resistant and highest yielding trees. Very occasionally these will be planted directly into the cleared forest, with several seeds sown in each growing site so that, after they are a few inches tall, all but the healthiest can be weeded away.

More common practice, though, is to start the cacao in a nursery. The seeds are planted in individual rush baskets set out in a simple, open-sided greenhouse. Cacao seeds germinate quickly, and in about half a year they are ready to be transplanted into the plantation. They are set down in their holes, rush baskets and all (the baskets will eventually decompose). Around the young trees may also be planted small, leguminous shade plants such as cassava or peppers, to give extra shelter to the young trees while, at the same time, providing the plantation owner with some crops while he waits for the cacao to reach maturity.

By their second year, the cacao trees may already be producing blossoms. In the third or fourth year, by which time they have topped six feet in height, some varieties produce pickable cacao pods. Almost all trees yield fruit by the time they are five years old, and by the age of ten they are fully producing, mature trees.

Although the ideal cacao climate would insure regular rainfall, most producing countries are naturally subject to varying degrees of seasonal fluctuation. Trees will still bear blossoms and pods at various stages of development; but most plantations have two regular seasons for harvesting crops. The major harvest in most cacao countries lasts from mid-autumn to early winter; a secondary harvest usually comes from mid-spring to early summer. In some countries, such as Java and the Dominican Republic, this schedule is reversed, with the main harvest coming from spring to summer; in other places, such as Nicaragua and Fernando Po, there is no secondary harvest; and in Mexico and some other countries, harvesting continues the year round, although there are months during which the larger part of the crop comes in.

Robert Louis Stevenson: Cacao Planter

Creating a cacao plantation is hard work. Although you can find romance in the idea of a tropical planter's life, the actual details of drudgery are enough to humble the most fanciful of dreamers. A case in point is the adventure writer Robert Louis Stevenson who, from 1890 to 1894, lived in Samoa as a cacao planter. Some of his experiences are, fortunately, set down in his correspondence with a friend, Sidney Colvin, who collected Stevenson's accounts in a volume known as the *Vailima Letters*:

"MY DEAR COLVIN,—This is a hard and interesting and beautiful life that we lead now. Our place is in a deep cleft of Vaea Mountain, some six hundred feet above the sea, embowered in forest, which is our strangling enemy, and which we combat with axes and dollars. I went crazy over outdoor work, and had at last to confine myself to the house, or literature must have gone by the board. *Nothing* is so interesting as weeding, clearing, and path-making; the oversight of labourers becomes a disease; it is quite an effort not to drop into the farmer; and it does make you feel so well. To come down covered with mud and drenched with sweat and rain after some hours in the bush, change, rub down, and take a chair in the verandah, is to taste a quiet conscience. And the strange thing that I mark is this: If I go out and make sixpence, bossing my labourers and plying the cutlass or the spade, idiot conscience applauds me; if I sit in the house and make twenty pounds, idiot conscience wails over my neglect and the day wasted."

Stevenson did finally manage to forge a sort of coexistence between his roles as writer and planter, as a later letter to Colvin shows:

"On Friday morning about eleven 1500 cacao seeds arrived, and we set to and toiled from twelve that day to six, and went to bed pretty tired. Next day I got about an hour

The romantic representation of a cacao plantation in this hundred-year-old engraving obscures the laborious drudgery necessary to raise a successful crop.

and a half at my History, and was at it again by 8.10, and except an hour for lunch kept at it till four P.M. Yesterday, I did some History in the morning, and slept most of the afternoon; and to-day, being still averse from physical labour, and the mail drawing nigh, drew out of the squad, and finished for press the fifth chapter of my History; fifty-nine pages in one month; which (you will allow me to say) is a devil of a large order; it means at least 177 pages of writing; 89,000 words! and hours going to and fro among my notes. However, this is the way it has to be done; the job must be done fast, or it is of no use. And it is a curious yarn. Honestly, I think people should be amused and convinced, if they could be at the pains to look at such a damned outlandish piece of machinery, which of course they won't. And much I care.

"When I was filling baskets all Saturday, in my dull mulish way, perhaps the slowest worker there, surely the most particular, and the only one that never looked up or knocked off, I could not but think I should have been sent on exhibition as an example to young literary men. Here is how to learn to write, might be the motto. You should have seen us; the verandah was like an Irish bog; our hands and faces were bedaubed with soil; and Faauma was supposed to have struck the right note when she remarked (*à propos* of nothing), 'Too much *eleele* (soil) for me!' The cacao (you must understand) has to be planted at first in baskets of plaited cocoa-leaf. From four to ten natives were plaiting these in the woodshed. Four boys were digging up soil and bringing it by the boxful to the verandah. Lloyd and I and Belle, and sometimes S. (who came to bear a hand), were filling the baskets, removing stones and lumps of clay; Austin and Faauma carried them when full to Fanny, who planted a seed in each, and then set them, packed close, in the corners of the verandah. From twelve on Friday till five P.M. on Saturday we planted the first 1500, and more than 700 of a second lot. You cannot dream how filthy we were, and we were all properly tired."

The Cacao Harvest

A cacao plantation ready for harvesting is an enchanting sight. One British writer in the nineteenth century gave this brief but eloquent description of his first sight of a Latin American plantation:

"The branches do not grow low, so that in looking down a piece of ground the vista is like a miniature forest hung with thousands of golden lamps—anything more lovely cannot be imagined."

But if the planter is going to make his living, he cannot be held in sway very long by the beauty that surrounds him. The lantern-like pods must be removed from the trees at the peak of ripeness.

Great care must be taken; remember that the cacao tree, though very tall, is also extremely delicate; any cuts in its

An African plantation hand expertly wields a knife or other special sharp implement to cut ripe cacao pods from their tree. Extreme care must be taken to harvest without damaging the delicate tree or other pods.

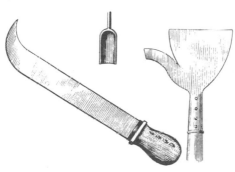

bark would be easy targets for one of the dreaded diseases already described. The pod stems secure the fruit to the tree fairly firmly; a shake will not bring them down. Plucking is no good, for it too can damage the tree. And precision is needed, for the ripe fruit may very well be right next to fragile blossoms or immature fruit. Finally, there is the problem of height: a good deal of the pods may be growing beyond a man's reach, yet the tree cannot support a ladder and the layout of the plantation discourages the use of any large, free-standing picking platforms.

All a good plantation worker needs are two simple tools. For the lower pods within his reach, he carries a heavy knife such as a machete. For the higher pods, cacao planters have developed a basic, but very sophisticated device: at the end of a long, lightweight but sturdy pole is lashed a wedge-shaped blade, from one side of which extends another blade shaped in a downward-curving hook. Depending on the angle at which the pod is growing, and how it is placed in relation to others, the worker can cut it down either by an upward thrust at the stem or by hooking the side blade around the stem and pulling down.

The picker must have a good eye, and a lot of experience. Because most plantations have a huge variety of different types of cacao, the pods of no two trees will show precisely the same signs of ripeness. He must watch for the first streaks of yellow or orange along the furrows of the pod, and know just when to cut it down. He must also be able to spot diseased and defective pods, so that they can be cut down and separated immediately from the healthy ones.

As the pickers proceed along the rows of trees, they are usually followed by women and children who carry on their heads baskets in which they gather up the fallen pods. Full baskets are carried to a clearing nearby, where the ripe pods are deposited in great heaps. As in the plantation ready for harvest, the profusion of pods is overwhelming; even people looking at the harvest from a technical viewpoint can get momentarily carried away. As Arthur W. Knapp, a

After the men cut down cacao pods using special harvesting tools, the women carry baskets full of pods (below left) to a clearing where they are deposited in huge piles (below). Each pod is broken open, the beans scooped out and the shell discarded.

research chemist for the British chocolate firm of Cadbury, wrote in 1920 in his book *Cocoa and Chocolate*:

"Once one has seen a great heap of cacao pods it glows in one's memory: anything more rich, more daring in the way of colour one's eye is unlikely to light on. The artist, seeking only an aesthetic effect would be content with this for the consummation and would wish the pods to remain un-broken."

Ancient Harvest Celebrations

A modern man may certainly marvel at the rich fruits of a successful cacao harvest. But nothing can compare to the celebrations of the Mayans following the harvest of their precious, god-given pods. Bancroft, in *The Native Races of the Pacific States of North America*, gave an account of the elaborate post-harvest ceremonies:

"As many as sixty persons, all men, though a number of them represented women, took part in a dance. They were painted of various colors and patterns, and wore upon their heads beautiful tufts of feathers, and about their person divers ornaments, while some wore masks like bird's heads. They performed the dance going in couples and keeping at a distance of three or four steps between pair and pair. In the centre of a square was a high pole of more than sixty feet in height driven firmly into the ground; on the top was seated a gaudily painted idol which they called the god of the *cacaguat*, or cacao; round the top were fixed four other poles in the form of a square, and rolled upon it was a thick grass rope at the ends of which were bound two boys of seven or eight years of age. One of them had in one hand a bow and in the other a bunch of arrows; the other boy carried a beautiful feather fan and a mirror. At a certain step of the

The Mayans held elaborate ceremonies (above) to celebrate their cacao harvest. Some sense of wonder in the tropical splendor of cacao even rubbed off onto civilized man, as can be seen in an early label (left) from the British firm of Cadbury.

dance boys came out from the square and the rope began to unroll; they went round and round in the air, always going further out and counterbalancing one another, the rope still unrolling. While they were descending, the sixty men proceeded with their dance to the sound of singers beating drums and tabors. The boys passed through the air with much velocity, moving their arms and legs to present the appearance of flying. When they reached the ground the dancers and singers gave some loud cheers and the festival was concluded. Another favorite amusement was a performance on a swinging bar. For this two tall forked posts were firmly planted in the ground; across them and resting in the forks a pole was strongly bound. This pole passed at right angles through a hole in the centre of a thick bar, made to revolve upon it and of very light wood; near the end of the bar were cross sticks for the performers to take hold of. A man placed himself at each end, and when the bar was set in motion they went tumbling round and round, to the delight of the spectators."

The Processing Commences: Fermentation

A while ago we left our description of the wondrous cacao tree before seeing what was actually inside its pods. Now, with the plantation workers, we are ready to have a look.

From the heap of pods a worker picks up a ripe cacao fruit. Holding it lengthwise across the palm of his hand, with the other hand he strikes the pod with a machete or a short, heavy stick. With one experienced blow the pod is split in half. (Experts can split as many as five hundred pods in an hour.)

Inside the shell, encased in a pulpy white, acidic fruit, are five rows of cacao beans, from twenty to forty in total. They are shaped like almonds, flat or slightly rounded; depending on what variety they are, they may be anything from a half to one and a quarter inches long, a half to three-quarters of an inch wide, and a third to half an inch thick. These beans will be made into cocoa and chocolate.

A woman expertly splits a cacao pod in two with a sharp knife (right). Inside are rows of cacao beans (below), surrounded by a pulpy white fruit. The pulp is acidic, and only long-experienced workers are able to remove the beans with their bare hands.

The women and children now scoop out the cacao beans, usually using a stick to avoid irritating their hands with the juice of the pulp. They strip off the membranes joining the rows of beans, and throw them away with the empty pod husks. The creamy beans, already turning purple through reaction with the air, are now ready for fermentation.

The cacao beans are heaped on the ground in large piles, or sometimes placed in large baskets or boxes, and covered with banana leaves or palm fronds. Bacteria react with the sugar in the pulp that securely surrounds each bean, converting it to alcohol and carbon dioxide and subsequently to acetic acid. Depending on the variety of bean, this process may continue for anywhere from two to nine days, during which time the heaps of beans are turned over often to make sure that they ferment evenly.

Fermentation is a critical process that accomplishes several things. Most basically, it loosens the pulp from the beans themselves. Further, as a chemical reaction it generates a great deal of heat—as much as 125° F—which kills off the germinating powers of the beans. And most important, the juices produced react with enzymes in the cacao beans, tempering their inherent bitter quality and developing color and flavor characteristics that will be brought out later during roasting. The beans, now a rich brown, are ready for the next stage in processing.

A pile of fermenting cacao beans is turned over (left) so the process affects all beans evenly. After two to nine days, the beans, now brown, are raked out in the sun to dry (below).

A Sunbath for the Beans

Although a good deal of the juices drain away during fermentation, half the weight of the cacao beans is still moisture. Before being sold and shipped, the beans must be dried in order to halt fermentation and to safeguard against rot and spoilage in storage—a danger already great enough in the humid heat of the tropics.

Drying is most simply accomplished by giving the beans a sunbath: spreading them out on wooden trays or bamboo mats and leaving them out in direct sunlight. This continues for up to two weeks, with the beans regularly mixed and turned as well as being picked over to remove any sticks, stones, and defective or germinating beans.

If the weather changes, the mats or trays can be carried into sheds for temporary shelter. Of course, because the ideal cacao climate requires regular rain, a lot of labor would then be expended on carrying the beans back and forth from sun to shed. An alternative method, much more convenient although not nearly as high in care or quality, is machine drying. At its simplest, this involves directing hot air pipes at the trays of beans. More sophisticated, diesel-driven apparatus can dry several tons of beans in less than a day. With drying completed, the beans are packed in jute sacks that hold from 130 to 200 pounds, and they are ready for market.

The World of Cacao Commerce

The most surprising thing about the sale of processed cacao is that, in reality, it has been sold while it is still safely hidden in pods clinging to the trees. Cacao is dealt on a "futures" market, in which the sale of set quantities of beans, at a mutually agreed upon price, is contracted as long as eighteen months before actual delivery.

It is true, though, that this agreement is not made directly with the cacao grower. In many countries where cacao is produced there exist central marketing boards, set up to protect the individual farmers from world price fluctuations beyond their control; these boards usually pay the farmer roughly half of the current world price, and the resulting profits to the board are expended on research and development in cacao agriculture and trade as well as on building cacao bean reserves as a hedge against drops in world cacao

Stacked more than thirty high, sacks of cacao beans – each weighing as much as two hundred pounds – are inspected by a warehouseman.

values. Some boards are run by the government, others are cooperatives, and still others are a compromise in which certain government controls are placed on a free-enterprise market. But all countries have the same very basic goal of trying to minimize the chance of losses and maximize gains.

In any case, the farmer's cacao beans will all follow the same general route. Once packed in their sacks, they are transported to a central buying station or shipping center. Here the beans are weighed and official inspectors assess their quality in order to assign them a price from the current sale. From each consignment of cacao the inspector takes a random sample of a few hundred beans. These he cuts in half, counting the number of beans with purple centers (a sign of incomplete fermentation), growths of mold, and various other defects that indicate some fault in their preparation. The total number of defects earns the cacao a quality rating which determines its price. The farmer is paid, and bids his cacao farewell.

Next, the beans are carried to the port from which they will ultimately be shipped to their final destination. Here they undergo the same careful assessment they had at the buying station, after which they are sold to merchants or manufacturers. While awaiting sale and shipment they are stored in special warehouses kept dry and at a constant temperature of around 80° F. Under such regulated conditions the cacao can be safely kept for several months.

Trading in Cacao Futures

In the heady mood of monetary speculation that followed the First World War, the price of cacao rose astronomically . . . until 1921, when the market in cacao beans crashed even more rapidly than it had soared. International traders in the commodity felt the need to organize a market exchange that would provide some regulatory framework for the buying and selling of cacao, enabling all those involved in the trade to limit the risks naturally inherent in a product whose price is so precariously linked to even the slightest fluctuations in world production.

The leader in this movement was the New York Cocoa Exchange, which was established in 1925. By setting up a marketplace for the sale of cacao on futures contracts, or futures—agreements to buy or sell set quantities of cacao beans at set prices on some date as far as eighteen months in the future—the exchange gives traders a sort of anchor for their transactions. Say, for example, a merchant buys a consignment of recently harvested cacao beans. He may safeguard his purchase by selling, on the New York Cocoa Exchange, the same quantity in futures at a suitable price. If the actual market price of the cacao he has purchased drops, he still has the set price on his futures contract to compensate.

In some parts of the world, harvested cacao still travels a hazardous route, such as the Ghanaian boat journey shown above left. Since the 1920s the commodity's movements, primitive or sophisticated, have been controlled by market exchanges such as the New York Cocoa Exchange, on whose modern, active trading floor (below) international transactions are carried out.

The exchange also provides special alternative trading opportunities for manufacturers, independent growers and trade boards. If cacao prices dip, manufacturers may take advantage of the situation by buying their future cacao supplies at a profitable price. Conversely, if the trading price rises, a grower or board may arrange for the sale of crops at this fixed price well before the pods are even picked from the trees.

There are people, not necessarily involved directly in the cacao trade, who use the New York Cocoa Exchange—as well as associate exchanges in London, Amsterdam, Hamburg and elsewhere—much as investors play the stock market. These speculators take long or short term risks on the purchase and sale of cacao stocks, within the securely regulated framework of the exchange. For such businessmen cacao probably holds a special romantic appeal beyond their profit sheets when their cacao transactions are over.

To the Magical Factory

No matter how the sale of cacao is transacted—no matter who is involved in its purchase—the ultimate destination of the cacao beans is the chocolate factory. Here the beans will undergo their complicated transformation into the various cocoa and chocolate products. To change cacao beans into the chocolate bar you purchase in a store, for example, requires seven or more complicated manufacturing steps that may take as many as four days.

Just imagine the rough-husked cacao beans and the smooth, delicious chocolate bar side by side. Some really magical things must go on inside the chocolate factory! And the imagination gets greater inspiration from the air that surrounds the factory walls: every breath brings the sweet aroma of chocolate, almost strong enough to taste by sticking out your tongue.

Chocolate is such an innocent delight that it would be wonderful to think that the inside of a chocolate factory was an amalgam of every other delight life has to offer. The British writer Roald Dahl created just such a place in his marvelous book *Charlie and the Chocolate Factory*:

"They were looking down upon a lovely valley. There were green meadows on either side of the valley, and along the bottom of it there flowed a great brown river.

"What is more, there was a tremendous waterfall halfway along the river—a steep cliff over which the water curled and rolled in a solid sheet, and then went crashing down into a boiling whirlpool of froth and spray.

"Below the waterfall (and this was the most astonishing sight of all), a whole mass of enormous glass pipes were dangling down into the river from somewhere high up in the ceiling! They really were *enormous*, those pipes. There must have been a dozen of them at least, and they were sucking up the brownish muddy water from the river and carrying it away to goodness knows where. And because they were made of glass, you could see the liquid flowing and bubbling along inside them, and above the noise of the waterfall, you could hear the never-ending suck-suck-sucking sound of the pipes as they did their work.

"Graceful trees and bushes were growing along the riverbanks—weeping willows and alders and tall clumps of rhododendrons with their pink and red and mauve blossoms. In the meadows there were thousands of buttercups.

"'*There!*' cried Mr Wonka, dancing up and down and pointing his gold-topped cane at the great brown river. 'It's *all* chocolate! Every drop of that river is hot melted chocolate of the finest quality. The *very* finest quality. There's enough chocolate in there to fill *every* bathtub in the *entire* country! *And* all the swimming pools as well! Isn't it *terrific*? And just look at my pipes! They suck up the chocolate and carry it away to all the other rooms in the factory where it is needed! Thousands of gallons an hour, my dear children! Thousands and thousands of gallons!'"

65

And of course, Willie Wonka goes on to tell them, everything in this Eden-like setting is edible, even the grass and the buttercups.

Sad to say, chocolate factories are not really like Willie Wonka's. But there is still wonder to be found there, although of a scientific and technical nature, and there is evidence too of great care and devotion that are demanded and deserved by the "Food of the Gods."

Special Quarters for the New Arrivals

Cacao beans are treated with love and care from the moment they arrive at the factory. It is not likely that they will go straight from the delivery truck into the processing machinery; so there are special accommodations prepared for them to make their wait as comfortable and danger-free as possible.

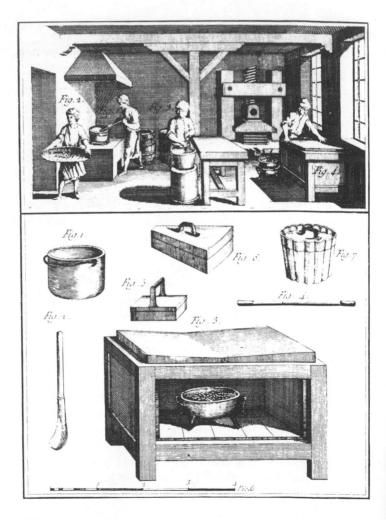

In the eighteenth century cocoa and chocolate manufacture was a small scale operation (left). Contrast this with a modern Dutch factory at Verkade, occupying a large part of the town of Zaandam.

There is danger, of course. In their own way, the cacao beans are as sensitive as their parent trees. If the temperature is too hot, stuffy and damp they may be subject to the growth of molds. Although their flavor properties are fairly hardy, they may deteriorate slightly under imperfect conditions; and any deterioration, no matter how slight, cannot be tolerated in an industry that prides itself on pure quality. The beans are also sensitive to foreign odors, which they can readily absorb.

So chocolate factories have, at the very least, separate warehouses for storing their cacao beans. These have carefully regulated atmospheres—cool, dry and well aired—in which the bags of cacao beans are stacked many times higher than a man.

More modern factories have changed over from simple warehouses to storage silos that may be higher than a hundred feet and hold upward of a thousand tons of beans. The beans are fed in from above by vacuum equipment, and then await automated conveyance into the factory.

Sprucing Up for Quality

Before the cacao beans begin their transformation into cocoa and chocolate, they must undergo a processing that will insure that they are at the peak of readiness. From the warehouse or silo, they are fed to a cleaning and sorting machine for this final sprucing.

Mixed with the cacao are bits of stone, pod, wood and fiber—final hangers-on from their long journey from the plantation. A controlled air current blows or vacuums away pieces lighter than the beans. Then another regulated current whisks the beans themselves away from heavier matter. And the beans are passed through a series of rotating brushes that remove anything still clinging to their surfaces.

Next, the beans are sorted. In the roasting that is to follow, it is important that the beans are treated in batches of uniform size. So they pass through a series of screens, each with holes slightly larger than the preceding one.

Finally, each batch is carefully assessed. Even in the most automated of factories, human judgment must be exercised to achieve the desired results. And every factory has its own secret formulas that bring more than a touch of old-fashioned skill and art to even the most modern of technologies.

Self-Realization Through Roasting

The cacao beans are now ready for the most important step in their progress through the factory, though far from their last. They move on to giant roasting machines that will change them from light brown, still relatively moist and bitter beans to dark, rich brown, dry beans with what we recognize as the aroma and flavor of chocolate.

There are two basic types of roaster. The older, more traditional but less convenient way is the batch roaster. As its name implies, it roasts beans in single batches, in large, rotating drums that are heated by flames or steam. The batch method takes anything from thirty minutes to two hours, depending on the results required, and the process is constantly under the eye of a master roasterman.

This time-consuming care is sacrificed for speed and efficiency in large, modern factories equipped with continuous-flow roasters. Just as the cacao beans traveled by conveyor belts from silo to, and through, cleaner and sorter, so they continue on the moving belt through these roasters, where blasts of heated air from all sides roast them in under half an hour. They then move on through streams of cooler air that halt the roasting process at just the right moment.

A small batch roaster stands ready to receive cacao beans through a chute from a storage area on the floor above.

In both methods, the critical roasting temperature is 250° F. Higher temperatures may be used for certain bean varieties or for specific effects. For example, more intensive roasting is used for beans destined to become cocoa powder, which requires stronger flavor and aroma; while chocolates of fine flavor and quality are made from beans of a lighter roast.

The heat generated for roasting the cacao beans does one more thing besides developing their flavor qualities. In spite of the cleaning they were given before they entered the roaster, the beans still had their tightly clinging shells. Since these husks are the first part of the beans to meet the heat of the roaster, they actually reach slightly higher temperatures than the denser, flavorful interiors. After roasting they are both brittle and loose—ready for easy removal. And, as you may have guessed, there is a machine that will remove them; but that machine is far more complicated, and does much more, than you would probably imagine.

Shell, Dust, Germ . . . and Nibs

Once the beans are roasted and cooled, a process of elimination begins. They are moved on to a machine usually known as a "cracker and fanner," which does precisely what its name says.

At the heart of this giant apparatus are conical, serrated rollers that revolve next to each other at a carefully regulated distance. The beans pass between them and are cracked into good-sized pieces. (If the cones were too close together, the beans would be crushed or pulverized, making it impossible to separate out the undesirable elements.

Now the fragments work their way down a series of graduated sieves that mechanically sort them by size. At each level, fans waft away the lightweight bits of shell and the inevitable dust produced during even the most careful cracking.

Another sort of fragment eliminated by the sieving is the dead germ, or tiny germinating shoot, of the cacao bean. Although these tiny, rod-shaped particles account for only about one percent of the total fragments passing through the cracker and fanner, after roasting they seem to hold a monopoly on bitterness. Unless they are removed, the final chocolate product cannot be really satisfactory. But the germs are hard and relatively heavy, and their distinctive shape makes it easy to screen them away into a separate collecting drum.

Although they have been drawn off, there is still value to be had from these discards. Of greatest importance is the cacao shell. First, a fat may be extracted from it which, although not as high in quality as that obtained from the bulk of the cacao bean (as we shall soon see), is still a good commercial vegetable fat product. Secondly, a chemical stimulant called theobromine is extracted; this may be used in the production of products ranging from cola drinks to pharmaceuticals. And the shell has also been found to be valuable as a soil mulch and as an additive or supplement to cattle feed.

From silo to the conclusion of cracking and fanning, the cacao beans have lost about 20 percent of their weight. So what is left after everything else has been eliminated? Only the essential ingredient in the manufacture of cocoa and chocolate: the many-sided fragments of cacao bean, now 99 percent pure, called "nibs."

Roasted cacao beans leave one type of continuous roasting machine, through which beans travel on a spiraling route.

Changing from Solid to Liquid

On move the cacao nibs, to the grindstone or mill. Soon these crisp little nuggets of roasted cacao bean will become the final, liquid raw material of cocoa and chocolate manufacture: chocolate liquor. The secret behind this alteration from a solid to a liquid state is a simple one: more than half of the nibs' total weight (53 to 54 percent) consists of the fat known as cocoa butter.

The nibs are fed between large grindstones, which give them a preliminary milling before they move on to a series

Dark brown roasted cacao beans await the removal of their brittle shells, which will be done in a cracking and fanning machine.

of heavy steel rollers which reduce them to a fine paste. The cell walls of the roasted cacao are broken down, releasing the cocoa butter; and the friction caused by grinding generates heat which melts the fat. The result is a dark brown, thick liquid—the chocolate liquor.

Three basic things may be done with the chocolate liquor. First, it can be poured into molds and cooled. These blocks of solidified chocolate liquor are familiar to us all as unsweetened, bitter, baking chocolate. But more likely than

not, the liquor will be destined for one of two other possible factory routes: it may be separated into cocoa powder and cocoa butter, or it may be transformed into fine eating chocolate.

Making Cocoa: A High-Pressure Job

The manufacture of cocoa is simpler, and less time-consuming, than that of chocolate. And its by-product, cocoa butter, is an essential ingredient of eating chocolate. So we will first follow a batch of chocolate liquor to the cocoa presses.

If you squeezed some chocolate liquor through a very fine cloth, you would be left with a more solid lump of brown cocoa inside the cloth, while an oil the color of molten butter oozed out. Although such an exercise demonstrates the basic principle behind the manufacture of cocoa, it also shows how much more sophisticated the factory equipment must be: it takes much more power than that of two human hands to squeeze out all the fat there is in a mass of chocolate liquor.

Hydraulic pressure must be used. The hot chocolate liquor flows into large, circular metal vats fitted with finely perforated filter bottoms. Hydraulic rams compress these vats, building up a pressure as high as six thousand pounds per square inch. Cocoa butter flows away, and a flat, circular, hard cake of solid cocoa is left behind.

This cocoa cake may be left with anything from 10 percent cocoa butter (classified as low-fat) to 22 percent or more (medium-fat), depending on what its commercial use will be. Low-fat cocoa usually goes to other food manufacturers, where it will be used as a flavoring for ice cream and other dairy goods, baked goods, and confections. Cocoa with a higher fat content usually finds its way to your kitchen as drinking chocolate.

Finally, the cakes of cocoa are conveyed to steel rollers that crush them into powder. This powder is then sifted by sieves or blowers; the fine particles of cocoa powder are sent off for packaging (or other processing to produce sweetened and creamy instant chocolate drinks), and the larger particles are sent back for another trip through the rollers.

The processing of cacao was a straightforward mechanical job in the mid-nineteenth century, as can be seen in an advertisement for a German milling machine (left). Modern factories require high-pressure machines such as the one below, which squeezes cocoa butter from chocolate liquor.

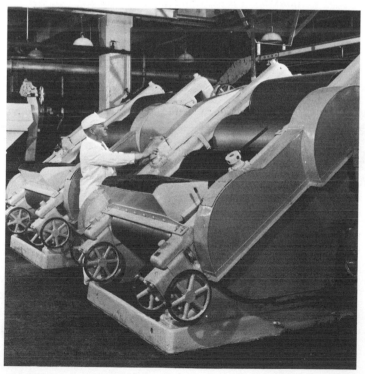

VAN HOUTEN'S PURE SOLUBLE COCOA

MARTIN CHUZZLEWIT.

best & goes farthest.

"I said to Mrs Harris, Mrs Harris says I try Van Houten's Cocoa"

"Copyright" by permission of Messrs Chapman & Hall, London.

Mrs. GAMP.

A Debt to the Dutch

Lovers of cocoa owe a large debt to the Dutchman C. J. van Houten, who invented the cocoa press in 1828. Van Houten is also responsible for developing the method known as "Dutching"—an alkalizing process that neutralizes the acidity of cocoa powder, making it more digestible, better in flavor, easier to mix with liquids, and darker in color. The alkalies do not, in fact, add a flavor of their own to the cocoa; rather, in reacting with the cocoa's natural acids, they produce traces of salt similar to those occurring naturally in other foods. About 90 percent of cocoa powders are Dutched, and their colors range from the light brown of the lightly treated to brownish-black, more thoroughly alkalized cocoa.

Butter That Never Saw a Cow

With all the attention received by cocoa, it is all too easy for us to forget its parted comrade, the cocoa butter. But the manufacturer pays careful attention to this product; cocoa butter is a remarkable commodity, with a great many important uses and a respectable commercial value.

After careful filtering, the cocoa butter squeezed from the presses sets to a color and consistency strikingly similar to dairy butter. Like butter, it remains solid at normal room temperatures, and melts at around 90° F—just the right temperature to melt in the mouth.

76

Cocoa butter also has excellent keeping properties. As long as it is kept cool it does not melt, and it can be stored for very long periods of time without oxidizing or going rancid. Its impeccable purity also makes it an important part of fat-based cosmetics and medications.

But it is its ability to melt in the mouth that is cocoa butter's most important quality, for the greatest bulk of cocoa butter goes into the manufacture of eating chocolate. On the average, 35 percent of the weight of a chocolate bar is cocoa butter. It is no wonder, then, that a common description of good chocolate is that it does, indeed, melt in your mouth.

The alkalizing process known as "Dutching" was invented by the Dutch firm of van Houten. Their milder, more soluble form of cocoa that resulted quickly won admirers in other countries, as can be seen from the late-nineteenth-century English labels shown here.

Teams of workers manned the mills and refiners in a French chocolate factory in the nineteenth century.

Mixing Together the Basic Ingredients

The manufacture of eating chocolate is not simply a matter of adding the right amount of cocoa butter to other in-gredients, mixing it all up and letting it harden. The pure and simple taste of chocolate is in fact the product of a complicated and conscientious manufacturing process.

We start with a batch of chocolate liquor, no different from the sort we have already seen changed under hydraulic pressure into cocoa and cocoa butter. Now, instead of having the cocoa butter extracted from it, more cocoa butter is added to the chocolate liquor. Powdered sugar is also added, usually making up from 40 percent of the total contents (for bittersweet chocolate) to about 60 percent (for the sweetest of chocolates). For milk chocolate, milk is of course added—in powdered form the equivalent of a glass of whole milk for each average-sized individual chocolate bar. And for the manufacture of elegant, creamy "white chocolate," milk and sugar are added to cocoa butter, without a trace of chocolate liquor.

All these ingredients are mixed in a machine traditionally called a *melangeur*, after the French for "mixer." Here rotating arms knead the ingredients together into a gritty substance with the texture of dough or paste. Indeed, at this stage it is called chocolate paste.

Chocolate Rolls Uphill

This chocolate paste would not be very pleasant to eat. It would be like chewing on chocolate-flavored gravel—not a very refined pastime. And refining is precisely what the chocolate paste will receive—by climbing through a refining mill.

This consists of at least three but often five or more steel rollers mounted horizontally one above the other. Each roller turns in the opposite direction from, and at a speed slightly faster than, the one below it. In this way the chocolate paste, which is fed to the bottom roller, adheres to it and revolves upwards, where it is not only ground against but also literally torn away by the next roller. The spacing between rollers decreases as the paste progresses upwards and is reduced to finer and finer particles. Of course, as we already know from the original grinding of the cacao nibs, such friction generates heat; but here, in order to keep the paste at a consistency that will allow it to be handled by the refiner, the rollers are cooled from within by water. When the chocolate is finally scraped off the top roller by a fixed blade, it consists of fine, dry flakes, with particles as small as thirty microns (only slightly bigger than one-thousandth of an inch).

Chocolate Gets the Shell Treatment

Even after refining has reduced the particles of the chocolate paste to minute uniformity, the mixture still has a texture similar to very fine sand. Nothing more can be done by the refining rollers, for they reduce the particle size only at the expense of giving them quite a battering and leaving them with microscopic but very rough edges.

The chocolate's sand-like texture is, in fact, a key factor in its further refinement. Think of the natural polishing action of the sea. As waves roll in and draw away, they carry with them countless grains of sand. If you have ever picked up a beach stone and run your fingers over its immensely pleasing, smooth contours, you have had first-hand experience of the work these water-borne sand grains can accomplish.

So the chocolate maker applies this same principle to his chocolate paste, putting the tiny, rough particles of chocolate mixture to work polishing each other. Had scientific analysis been able to show Rodolphe Lindt, the Swiss chocolate manufacturer who first developed this process towards the end of the last century, that this is in fact what happens, it might have simply been called polishing. But the actual reason for the effect remained a bit of a mystery until much more recently, and so instead this final refinement is called "conching," taking its name from the French word *conche*, because of the shell-like curve of the trough in which it takes place.

The conches are long troughs with curved bottoms, which can hold as much as a ton of chocolate paste. (And some more modern rotary conches can hold over two tons.) They are heated to a temperature of between 120 and 190° F, keeping the chocolate in a fairly fluid state. A giant roller continually plows back and forth through the trough,

A giant roller plows through a trough of molten chocolate in the final refining process of conching.

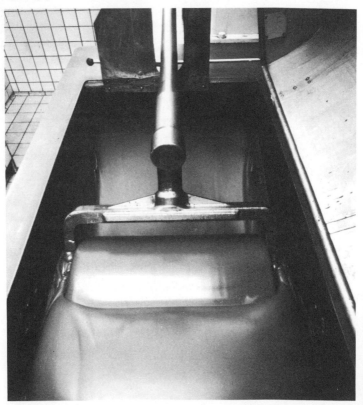

turning the chocolate over and over (and more or less simulating a wave-like motion). In this way, the particles continually rub against each other, smoothing away their rough edges. And a certain amount of air is incorporated into the chocolate by the churning, making it lighter while developing its aroma and flavor.

More cocoa butter is usually added during the three days or more during which conching continues. Flavoring agents are also added at this late stage, the most common being vanilla, which adds a further smoothness and delicacy of taste.

When conching is finished, the chocolate maker has, in the liquid state, a batch of true fondant or melting chocolate.

How Chocolate Keeps Its Temper

After conching, chocolate is in taste and texture the product we all recognize. But it is, of course, still in a hot liquid state; and if its transformation from liquid to solid is not handled with proper care, a lot of the quality that has been developed in it through conching will be lost.

This is guarded against through tempering, the final preparatory process before the actual formation of the chocolate products. Tempering is basically concerned with cooling the chocolate down to a more manageable state while still keeping it entirely homogenous. Tempering machines are large vats containing rotary stirring arms and enveloped by water-cooled jackets. While the stirring arms revolve, the temperature of the chocolate is slowly and steadily reduced to around 86° F—just cool enough for the liquified cocoa butter content to reach a malleable, plastic state.

The chocolate is now ready to be molded or otherwise shaped into many familiar confectionary items.

Shake, Rattle and Roll

The best-known and most widely sold chocolate product is undoubtedly the chocolate bar. In the chocolate manufacturing trade this is referred to as molded chocolate. And classed with the molded products are those containing "coarse-grain additives"—nuts to you, whole or crushed, or candied fruits, puffed cereals, raisins, flavored sugar chips and other serendipitous delights, which are blended into the batch of tempered chocolate just before molding begins.

The tempered chocolate, now having the consistency of a loose dough, is transferred to a pouring machine. A line of nozzles carefully pours measured amounts of the chocolate into brightly polished metal molds which march beneath the nozzles on a conveyor belt.

Modern chocolate bars with nuts come out of shiny metallic, assembly line molds (above) – a far cry from the small, semi-automated French machine (below) exhibited in London in 1851.

It is very important that the chocolate completely fills the molds. After all, you would not like to unwrap a bar to discover its surface riddled with bubbles and gaps. To make sure that this does not happen, the conveyor belt carries the chocolate molds to a shaking line. In place of the round rollers that normally keep the belt moving smoothly, bumpy rollers are used for this part of the trip; these cause a great deal of vibration and jumping. At this stage, a careful look at the lines of molds would show countless air bubbles rising to their surfaces and bursting.

This bumpy road passed, the conveyor carries the molds on to the cooling chamber, where cold air currents cause the chocolate to solidify. As it does so, it contracts slightly; so when the molds move out of the cooling chamber they are automatically inverted, given a final gentle shake, and the gleaming, perfectly formed chocolate bars are then deposited on the belt, ready to be moved on to the wrapping equipment.

Fillings, Coatings and Spinning Bunnies

Regular chocolate bars are the simplest products to manufacture. Much more complicated equipment exists to produce a wide variety of chocolate novelties.

The most basic of these are filled chocolate bars, usually marked off into a series of squares or rectangles each containing some creamy, liquid or solid filling. These begin in the same way as the solid chocolate bars, but as soon as the tempered chocolate is poured, the molds are inverted, leaving a coating of chocolate that follows their contours. The molds are then moved to the cooling chambers.

These hardened chocolate shells, still in the molds, then travel to another machine that automatically deposits an exact amount of filling in each indentation. Then another layer of chocolate is poured over the molds, and back they go for a final cooling. The molds are then inverted, and whole filled chocolate bars are deposited, ready for wrapping.

Filled bars are, in a sense, a very pedestrian version of the more elegant, individual chocolate-covered candies. These are traditionally hand-dipped products (and you will find some basic instructions for dipping your own creations in the next chapter). But modern technology has long since found a way to mass produce them.

First of all, centers must be made. Truffles, nougats, crème fondants, nutty croquants, marzipans and the like are manufactured and then cut to exact shapes by a cutting press that sends them down the conveyor belt in neat, uniform files.

A pedestrian stops to admire an elaborate Easter egg in the window of the renowned confectioners Floris in London.

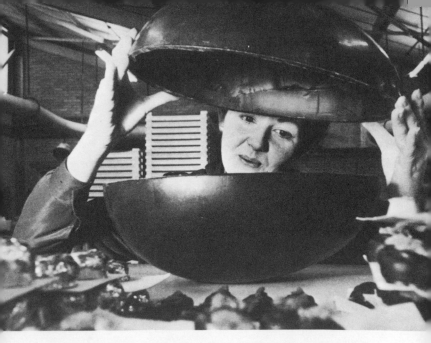

A factory inspector checks the quality of a giant molded Easter egg (above). Modern molding techniques make it possible to create shapes such as bunnies (above right) and the letters traditionally presented in Holland on St. Nicholas' Day (below right)

Liquid centers are made in an especially interesting way. It stands to reason that they cannot be die-cut like other centers. Sheets of a starchy powder are laid out on wide trays. Regularly spaced, small indentations are made in the powder. Then a machine pours a hot mixture of sugar syrup and the liquid filling into each little crater. Over two days or so, the mixture cools in such a way that the sugar separates and forms a crust that completely surrounds the liquid. The starch powder is blown away and, once again, neat files of centers are carried along the conveyor belt.

The destination of all these centers, solid and liquid, is an apparatus known as an enrober—a delicate name for a machine that accomplishes what used to be the occupation of young girls. The belt passes the centers on to a moving grating that carries them through a continuously flowing curtain of molten chocolate, which can be regulated so that it makes up anything from 10 to 60 percent of each morsel's total weight. Some high-class candies are passed through the curtain twice, and may then continue to pass under nozzles that embellish them with delicate squiggles and other patterns.

Still more elegant chocolate delights are the hollow chocolate shapes that appear in the stores around festival times: delicate Easter bunnies and stalwart Santas, sometimes filled with an assortment of small wrapped chocolates

or with toy surprises. One very basic way of making these shapes is similar to the making of filled bars. Chocolate is poured into two mirror-image half-molds, which are inverted and then cooled to leave shells. The edges of the halves are then carefully heated, and the two halves joined together (any surprises having been inserted just before, of course).

A much more exciting method employs centrifugal force. Full-figure molds project on a rotating arm from a large cylinder that itself rotates. Molten chocolate is injected into the mold, which spins on its own axis while also being spun round the cylinder, causing the chocolate to be flung against every crevice and extremity. The molds are cooled, and then opened to reveal perfectly formed, hollow chocolate figures.

Molded for Melodrama

Chocolate can be molded to such perfection that at times chocolate shapes may be incredibly deceiving. There is no doubt that countless tricks have been played with chocolate shapes: paying a friend with foil-covered chocolate coins, offering smokers chocolate cigarettes, placing chocolate mice where the unsuspecting and easily scared may stumble upon them. And there is a great deal of melodramatic potential in molded chocolate guns, as was recognized in a simple Swiss poem dating from the early nineteenth century:

Young Jacob holds a pistol in his hand,
And says, "I'll kill myself my dear Susanne,
Unless you say you'll marry me as planned."
She stares, aghast, as the cool tempered man
Serenely holds the pistol to his head.
The girl cries, "Stop!" But Jacob seems upset:
The trigger's pulled . . .
                        Instead of dropping dead,
He eats the gun: it's only chocolate!
He chuckles as he chews it like a gangster.
No wonder she won't wed this foolish prankster.

Quality Control and Secret Plans

We have had a close look at the various stages in the manufacture of chocolate, watching it as it moves from one intricate machine to another. But let us now draw back a bit, to take in the chocolate factory as a whole.

Every stage of chocolate's progress through the modern factory is carefully controlled. Computerized panels regulate each machine, mixing ingredients to proportions coded on punched cards, controlling temperatures of conches and tempering vats, making sure that everything flows smoothly from one operation to the next.

Hand in hand with this carefully orchestrated control is the high standard of sanitation and hygiene to be found in chocolate factories. This certainly has something to do with the fact that most governments lay down strict health regulations; the United States Food and Drug Administration, for example, sets forth strict regulations on chocolate and cocoa ingredients, specifying obligatory minimum contents of chocolate liquor and, for milk chocolate, milk powder.

But beyond these legislative standards, surely there is a pride (and a profit) to be had from making the finest, purest chocolate possible. Chocolate manufacturers set their own standards beyond those government minimums. An important part of the chocolate factory that we did not see as we followed the manufacturing process is the testing laboratory. Checks are made on the chocolate at every stage of its production; new shipments of beans are inspected by microbiologists, nutritional experts pay attention to the quality and relative quantities of ingredients, chemists test the acidity of the roasted beans and the purity of the cocoa butter.

Efforts are always being made by the factory to improve its chocolate. It is a competitive business, and the research and development of new recipes and methods are subject to a very high degree of secrecy. Formulas and procedures for products currently on sale are closely guarded. (And automation helps here, minimizing the number of talkative humans who come in contact with these secrets.) Elsewhere in the factory grounds there are whole laboratories and small, self-contained manufacturing equipment devoted to work on possible new projects. Here the spark of an idea in a scientist's or technician's mind may be turned into a popular chocolate product two years or maybe ten years from now.

More like the control panel for a space shot than a chocolate confection, the dials and meters of a production line in an English factory are read and adjusted by a technician.

Chapter 3
Chocolate in Your Home

A great array of chocolate products are available to the modern consumer, including chocolate flakes that look as tempting on a slice of ordinary bread as they do atop a cake or a sundae.

Facts and Instructions

Diversions

A Cautionary Introduction

A courtier of King Louis XIII of France embraced the vogue for chocolate as eagerly as he embraced any courtly maiden who was naive enough to succumb to his charms. One day, a lady in waiting to the queen discovered that this suitor had, in addition to his usual presents of the finest drinking chocolate, given her another, unexpected, gift. She was pregnant.

The young woman was delighted. After all, she loved the courtier; and she fully expected that marriage would follow.

She quickly learned otherwise when her lover made it clear she was now a burden he would in future do without. The young woman decided that, if she could not have marriage, she would at least have revenge.

A week later, she wrote to her former lover, gaily announcing that it had all been a false alarm, and seductively inviting him to share her bed the following evening.

They ended their night of love in the usual manner: while he lay in bed, she retired to the kitchen to brew for him a steaming cup of chocolate. Only this time she added poison.

Her suitor quickly drained the cup, and as he put it down a puzzled expression crossed his face. But he did not have long to puzzle; the poison rapidly took effect.

With a huge effort he pulled his lover and murderer close to him

"About that chocolate," he gasped. "Next time be sure to add extra sugar to counteract the bitterness of the poison."

This chapter offers guidelines, not for people with such gruesome goals, but for those who need advice simply to insure that their everyday use of cocoa and chocolate achieves the desired perfection.

Even the elegant beauty of this eighteenth-century French chocolate service cannot conceal a bad cup of cocoa. Make sure you know the right way to brew it.

Some Chocolate Definitions

There are so many different types of cocoa and chocolate products on the market, not to mention a good number of items that you might *think* are cocoa or chocolate, that it is useful to have some idea of what means what. Here is a brief rundown on what you should expect these products to be:

Bitter, unsweetened or baking chocolate. Processed chocolate in its most basic form—the hardened mass of chocolate "liquor" produced when roasted nibs of cacao beans have been ground.

Semisweet, sweet or plain chocolate. Made from chocolate liquor to which sugar and cocoa butter are added according to the manufacturer's formula, then further refined to a smoother texture. Rough proportions of ingredients are a third each of chocolate, cocoa butter and sugar.

Milk chocolate. Made from chocolate liquor, condensed or powdered milk or cream, cocoa butter and sugar, and then refined to its familiar smoothness. This is the most widely eaten of chocolates, and manufacturers jealously guard their precise ingredient measures and processes used for making quality milk chocolate.

White "chocolate". In fact, not technically chocolate, because it contains no chocolate liquor—but delicious nonetheless. Made from cocoa butter (which has been separated from the chocolate liquor and then purified of any trace of cocoa), milk, sugar and vanilla and other flavorings.

Cocoa. The basic term for the solid, relatively fat-free mass left after cocoa butter has been squeezed away from chocolate liquor in a cocoa press. It contains anywhere from about 10 (low-fat) to 22 percent (medium-fat) cocoa butter. It is ground into fine cocoa powder, and may have sugar, milk or cream powder, and other flavorings and ingredients added to produce an "instant" cocoa or chocolate drink mix.

Cocoa or chocolate flavor. Watch out for this designation, and check the label to see what, in fact, the flavor comes from. Government regulatory bodies specify standards for minimum chocolate or cocoa contents; but it may be that, by using that word "flavor," the manufacturer is getting away with using artificial flavoring and coloring substances.

"Diet chocolate". This may fall under the heading of artificially flavored or at the very least artificially sweetened, chocolate. Chocolate made with artificial sweeteners in place of sugar can often taste diabolically bad. Some "diet" chocolates, however, are just chocolates with a low sugar and cocoa butter content: somewhat bitter and dry and brittle, but real chocolate. Check the label carefully before you buy.

Taking Care of Cocoa and Chocolate

Have you ever unwrapped a chocolate bar and found its surface covered with a light, powdery film? You may have thought it had gone bad, but if you ventured to eat it you probably found that nothing much was wrong with the taste except, perhaps, for a bit of brittleness and a slight lack of the accustomed smoothness. This was a bar with a case of "bloom."

Bloom cannot hurt you. It merely means that the chocolate has been improperly stored at too high a temperature, and some slight percentage of the cocoa butter has separated out and risen to the surface of the bar. The best storage temperature for chocolates is between 55° and 65° F (12 to 18° C), and it should never really go above 70° F (21° C). Bloom occurs as 80° F (26° C) is approached. At the same time, remember that if you refrigerate chocolate it will harden and require some time to return to a cool room temperature before being eaten. It is best to store it in a cool cupboard away from direct sunlight or sources of heat.

Cocoa requires the same temperature range as chocolate, but it has the additional need of relatively low humidity (around 50 percent). Since most of its fat has been removed, nothing like bloom affects it; but it can lose some of its color and its fine powdery texture if not stored in the correct way. This will not affect taste, but it may make the cocoa more difficult to measure and mix.

Finally, both chocolate and cocoa are sensitive to the odors of other foods, and can readily absorb them. So always keep them well wrapped (an airtight container for the cocoa will also help guard against the humidity). If you do not, you may find your cocoa or chocolate smelling or tasting of that fish you cooked last night, or the gas from the kitchen stove, or the piece of cheese in the refrigerator.

Chocolate comes in a vast variety of blends, shapes and sizes from manufacturers worldwide who make products designed to suit just about every imaginable taste.

lacta café

POULAIN

chocolat au lait

Poulain

au café

85 gram   3 oz

diabetic Plain Chocolate

ELITE

MILK

CHOCOLAT

1875–1975
le premier chocolat au lait du monde,
Daniel Peter inventeur.

gala peter

mi-doux · halbsüss

Making Substitutions

Every lover of chocolate and cocoa should naturally have close at hand ample quantities of both. But inevitably the time will come when you require one for cooking and find that you only have the other.

Do not despair. There are simple procedures for substituting one for the other. They are:

For chocolate, when you only have cocoa Remember that cocoa and chocolate were the same thing, until cocoa butter was removed to make the cocoa or added to make the chocolate. You can more or less undo what the chocolate factory has done by adding to the cocoa some sort of fat to make up for what was taken away. To substitute for one ounce (25 grams) of unsweetened chocolate, combine 2 level tablespoons of cocoa with 1 rounded teaspoon of cocoa butter or (since you probably will not have that on hand if you do not have the chocolate) vegetable shortening or butter. If a semisweet chocolate is required, add 2 tablespoons or so of sugar.

For cocoa, when you only have chocolate Cocoa is more concentrated in flavor. For drinks, use half again as much chocolate as you would cocoa.

A Cup of Cocoa

There is one secret step that almost everyone ignores when making a cup of cocoa. The magic word is "whisking," and it can make an amazing difference to the quality of your cupful. For each cup you need:

1 heaped teaspoon cocoa
1½ heaped teaspoons sugar

2 tablespoons hot water
a bit less than a cup of milk

In a saucepan combine the cocoa and sugar, and stir in the hot water. Continuing to stir, heat until it boils. Then add the milk and reduce the heat slightly. Heat the mixture thoroughly, but do not boil it. Remove from the heat.

Now, with a wire whisk or a rotary beater, give the drink a thorough beating for about fifteen seconds—until it is foamy. This accomplishes three things: it prevents any unpleasant skin forming on the surface of the cup; it fully incorporates all the particles into a smooth whole; and it actually develops the flavor of the drink, resulting in the most delicious cup of cocoa you have ever tasted. So, no matter what other ingredients you may add to make any hot chocolate drink, always beat it.

A cocoa vendor at his most mobile comes equipped with cups and spouts for four different blends, in this nineteenth-century French engraving based on a work by Gavarni.

Melting Chocolate

Although we consume it in many forms and as an ingredient in many different things, the basic image that the word "chocolate" brings to mind is a chocolate bar or other solid lump. Transforming that into something that will combine with other dry or liquid ingredients, or into a coating for a variety of confections, requires knowledge and care— although it need not be difficult.

Two adverse things may happen if an attempt is made to melt chocolate incorrectly. Direct heat can easily scorch chocolate, destroying both appearance and taste. And too high a heat can cause a milk chocolate to stiffen, making it difficult—if not impossible—to work with.

The simplest way to melt chocolate is over a pan of hot water. Fill a large, shallow saucepan with a couple of inches of water and place it on the burner. While the water is coming to a boil, take a smaller saucepan or a heatproof bowl and break the chocolate up into it. As soon as the water in the large pan is boiling, remove it from the heat, and place the vessel containing the chocolate into the water. The water should supply just the right amount of heat to melt the chocolate in a few minutes. Stir the molten chocolate to achieve uniform smoothness.

It is essential that no moisture comes into contact with the melting chocolate, for it will cause the chocolate to stiffen. If this happens, add a teaspoon or so of corn oil and stir the chocolate until it returns to its manageable molten state.

If you have an oven that you can regulate to a heat below 110° F (about 45° C), you can also melt chocolate there. Just break the chocolate into an ovenproof pan and pop it in for about an hour, making sure, when you do, that the pan does not come into very close contact with the source of heat. This achieves, in a carefully controlled way of course, the same effect you would get from leaving a bar of chocolate outdoors on a very hot day.

Finally, if your recipe calls for the chocolate to be mixed with a liquid, you can simply melt them together in a saucepan, using direct heat. Just be sure to keep the heat low and to stir constantly to insure even blending.

Shaping Chocolate

Chocolate is often used not only as an ingredient but also as a delicious decoration. Here are some simple rules to follow for shaping chocolate.

The easiest, least complicated chocolate decoration is grated chocolate. There is no need to tell you how to use a grater, but there is a small trick that will enable you to grate

Several thousand pounds of cocoa and chocolate supplied by the British firm of Cadbury were carried on an expedition in search of the North Pole, as depicted in this early advertisement.

chocolate more easily: an hour or so before grating, pop the chocolate into the refrigerator. Then, when the time comes to use it, you have a cold and absolutely solid block that is less likely to clog your equipment.

Another very popular chocolate shape is the curl. For this you need a block of chocolate at warm room temperature and a vegetable parer. Gently warm the parer blade—it should not be so hot that you cannot touch it—and draw it smoothly across the flat (that is, usually the bottom) side of the chocolate block.

You can make more elaborate chocolate shapes using molten chocolate. Melt the chocolate in one of the ways outlined in the preceding section. Then, continuing to stir it, let it slowly cool to a point at which it remains molten but may be comfortably touched. Spread a sheet of nonstick or wax paper on your kitchen counter and pour the chocolate onto the paper, distributing it evenly and thinly with a spatula or palette knife. When the surface of the chocolate begins to cloud slightly, it is setting; at this point, using a knife or a metal cutting shape, press down into the chocolate to make your shapes. Then let the chocolate fully set, and carefully lift your decorations from the paper.

Still another project is making your own chocolate Easter eggs. First you must empty eggshells, either by puncturing the wide end of a raw egg and shaking out its contents, or by carefully puncturing both ends and gently blowing the shell empty. Then melt chocolate in the usual way, and roll a sheet of heavy duty paper into a cone-shaped funnel. When the molten chocolate has cooled slightly, pour it into the funnel and carefully squeeze it into the eggshell (making certain that you have sealed one of the holes if you used the two-hole method for emptying it). Allow it several hours to set, and either decorate the shell with food colors or present it as a hardboiled egg to some unsuspecting friend.

Creating Simple Chocolate Confections

Perhaps the greatest delight in working with chocolate comes from making your own chocolate-based or chocolate-covered confections. The making of various coated chocolates is in fact a fairly complicated science to which books longer than this have been devoted in their entirety.

But you can derive a great deal of enjoyment from trying some of the few simple confections that follow; and you may be inspired to go on and teach yourself how to make chocolates that will rival those sold in the finest of shops.

Nut, Fruit, or Fruit-and-Nut Clusters

These are the least involved, and to some people the most satisfying, of homemade chocolate treats. Simply melt, in the usual manner, a desired quantity of chocolate; and add to it an equal amount of roasted nuts (unsalted), or preserved or candied fruits (raisins are the classic), or a mixture of both. Mix well, and spoon small clusters onto waxed paper or into individual frilled paper candy casings. Allow an hour or so for them to set.

Basic Dipped Chocolates

A dipped chocolate is a confection center—ranging from simple nuts or candied fruits to more complicated preparations—that has been carefully dipped in molten chocolate. Professionals use a very fine dipping chocolate known by the French word *couverture*, "covering," which has a slightly higher cocoa butter content than normal chocolates and sets to a fine, shiny glaze. This chocolate is available from most confectionery suppliers (check your classified directory); but as a beginner you are probably best off working with a supply of regular semisweet or milk chocolate.

You will also need a dipping fork, for handling the delicate, freshly dipped chocolates without leaving your indelicate fingerprints on them. You can purchase one from the same specialist shop that sells *couverture*; or you can easily make one from a long, strong piece of wire with a small loop at one end on which the chocolates can sit; or even a simple palette knife (which, as we have already seen, you can also use for making chocolate shapes).

Dipping is an easy, though delicate, operation. Chocolate should be melted in the usual way, and then allowed to reach the point at which it is cool to the touch but still quite liquid. The centers are then placed, one at a time, in the chocolate. When they are completely coated, the dipping tool is used to lift them from the bowl of chocolate, a gentle tap is given against the side of the bowl to shake away excess chocolate, and the chocolate is carefully placed on a sheet of nonstick paper or in its own individual paper cup.

You can dip whole roasted Brazil nuts or almonds in this way; or pieces of glacé fruit; or even carefully drained pieces of fresh or canned fruit such as chunks of pineapple or pitted cherries. Or you can begin to get more sophisticated, and make a basic but very versatile cream center.

A young worker in a chocolate factory uses a dipping fork to carefully drip a decorative pattern onto a dipped confection.

Basic Cream Centers

For about two dozen basic cream centers you need:

2 cups (250 grams) icing   1 egg white, beaten
  sugar
condensed milk

Slowly sift the sugar into the egg white, stirring continually. If it gets a bit too stiff while you are adding the sugar, moisten with a little condensed milk. Once all the sugar has been added, knead to stiff doughy consistency. Add a few drops of natural flavoring essences—vanilla, peppermint, coffee or whatever your favorite may be—while blending. Roll out on nonstick paper, cut patties with a cutting mold, and give them a day or so to set before covering as above.

Two pieces of chocolate ephemera represent the variety available to collectors at many antique stalls and shops: chocolate cards that used to, and in some cases still do, accompany chocolate bars; and old decorative cocoa tins; this example is from the turn of the century.

Inspirations

Information

Frivolities and Pastimes

CHOCOLAT FÉLIX POTIN

Le Cacaoyer. — *Chocolat. Cacao. Bonbons.*

The Other Sides of Chocolate

We have seen how chocolate progressed from a primitive drink and food of ancient Latin American tribes—a part of their religions, commerce and social life—to a drink favored by the elite of European society and gradually improved until it was incomparably drinkable and, later, superbly edible. We have also followed its complex transformation from the closely packed seeds of the fruit of an exotic tree to a wide variety of carefully manufactured cocoa and chocolate products. We have reviewed some of the simple rules by which these products can be used to perfection in the home; and in the next chapter we will sample the imaginative uses to which cocoa and chocolate are put in kitchens of many countries throughout the world.

But beyond the historical, the agricultural and commercial, and the culinary sides to chocolate, there are other facets not immediately apparent but certainly of potentially great interest to the chocolate connoisseur. For example, chocolate has an affect on both our health and our beauty; and in turn, it inspires or contributes to man's creation of beauty in literature and the arts. This chapter highlights some of the lesser known but very fascinating aspects of chocolate.

Chocolate, Health and Nutrition

In 1648, in his *A New Survey of the West Indies*, the Englishman Thomas Gage summed up nicely early thoughts on the physical effects of chocolate:

"True it is, it is used more in the *India*'s, than in the *European* parts, because there the Stomachs are more apt to faint than here, and a Cup of Chocolatte well confectioned comforts and strengthens the Stomach. For my self I must say, I used it twelve years constantly, Drinking one Cup in the morning, another yet before Dinner between nine or ten

*In the nineteenth century some cocoas prepared by the Dutch process,
which neutralized acidity, were billed as "health cocoa".*

of the clock; another within an hour or two after Dinner,
and another between four and five in the afternoon; and
when I was purpos'd to sit up late to study, I would take
another Cup about seven or eight at night, which would
keep me waking till about midnight. And if by chance I did
neglect any of these accustomed hours, I presently found my
stomach fainty. And with this custom I lived 12 years in
those parts healthy, without any obstructions, or oppilations, not knowing what either Ague or Feaver was. Yet
will I not dare to regulate by mine own, the Bodies of others,
nor take upon me the skill of a Physician, to appoint and
define at what time and by what persons this Drink may be
used. Only I say, I have known some that have been the
worse for it, either for Drinking it with too much Sugar,
which hath relaxed their Stomachs, or for Drinking it too
often. For certainly if it be drunk beyond measure, not only
this Chocolatte but all other drinks, or meats, though of
themselves they are good and wholesom, they may be
hurtful. And if some have found it oppilative, it hath come
by the too much use of it; as when one drinks over much
wine, instead of comforting and warming himself, he breeds
and nourisheth cold diseases, because nature cannot over-
come it, nor turn so great a Quantity into good nourishment.
So he that drinks much Chocolatte, which hath fat parts,
cannot make distribution of so great a Quantity to all the
parts; and that part which remains in the slender veins of
the liver must needs cause oppilations and obstructions. But
lastly to conclude with this *Indian* drink, I will add what I
have heard Physicians of the *India*'s say of it, and have seen

107

it by experience in others (though never I could find it in my self) that those that use this Chocolatte much, grow fat and Corpulent by it: which indeed may seem hard to believe. . . ."

Still other early writers on chocolate concentrated on the properties ascribed to it by the Indians. Bancroft, for example, recorded several medical uses in his *Native Races of the Pacific States*. Sometimes, he noted, these were closely related to religious ritual: "The bones of giants dug up at the foot of the mountains, were collected by their dwarfish successors, ground to powder, mixed with cacao, and drunk as a cure for diarrhea and dysentery." At other times, the cure was more direct: "Cacao, after the oil had been extracted was considered to be a sure preventive against poison." And the physical benefits of chocolate were not confined solely to medical problems; it was recognized early as an energy food: "This drink was nutritious, refreshing, and cooling, and was especially a favorite with those called upon to perform fatiguing labor with scant food."

These observations were, perhaps, best crystallized in the writings of the German naturalist Alexander von Humboldt, who observed that chocolate was unique in encompassing, in such a small space, a great deal of those elements essential to good nutrition and health. And modern science has confirmed the opinions of Humboldt and those earlier writers.

What, in fact, are the essentials provided by chocolate? Laboratory analysis has shown significant amounts of the following nutritional elements: thiamine, riboflavin, calcium, iron, and vitamins A and D. A one-ounce bar provides about 4 percent of an adult's daily protein needs (a sizeable amount for its weight), and rich supplies of carbohydrate and fat.

True, diet-conscious people shy away from foods that are rich in these last two ingredients. But it is because of its carbohydrate and fat content that chocolate is such a superb energy food. Napoleon was an early devotee of chocolate for this reason; he carried it with him on all his campaigns.

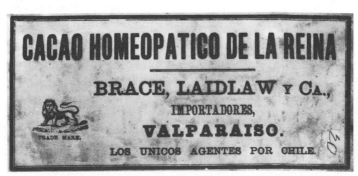

CACAO HOMEOPATICO DE LA REINA

BRACE, LAIDLAW y Ca.,

IMPORTADORES,

VALPARAISO.

LOS UNICOS AGENTES POR CHILE.

TRADE MARK.

Science was called in to lend support to cocoa advertising in the nineteenth century. A Chilean product (below left) was labeled "homeopathic," and a wise old chemist assured buyers of the purity of one English brand over all others (above).

More recently, soldiers in the Second World War relied on chocolate bars as a key element of their battle rations. Athletes find particularly good sustenance in chocolate during long workouts. And astronauts have chocolate as part of a diet specially designed to keep their energies at a peak during their taxing days or weeks in space.

Chocolate is quick, concentrated energy, satisfying and easily digested. And who says it cannot be eaten on a diet? That one-ounce bar contains only about 150 calories, more soothing to the cravings of a weight-watcher than a whole ton of celery sticks. If you count your calories carefully, why not include among your daily rations that single, small bar of chocolate? Nibble it slowly, savoring it morsel by morsel, and you will not only increase your enjoyment of it but, at the same time, start to build some of the will power so crucial in weight control.

A Healthy Epicure's Summation

The last word on chocolate and health deserves to be had by
the great nineteenth-century French epicure Jean Anthelme
Brillat-Savarin, author of the famous tome on food and
eating, *The Physiology of Taste or Meditations on Transcen-
dental Gastronomy*. He gives unarguable rules for living and
thriving with chocolate, presented here in the superb
modern translation by M. F. K. Fisher:

"Some people complain that they cannot digest chocolate;
some, on the other hand, insist that it does not satisfy them
and that it digests too quickly.

"It is quite possible that the first have only themselves to
blame, and that the chocolate they use is either of inferior
quality or badly prepared; for good well-made chocolate can
be assimilated by any stomach which can still digest even
feebly.

"As to the others, the remedy is easy: they should
fortify themselves at breakfast with a little meat pie, a cutlet,
or a skewered kidney; then they should drink down a good
bowl of the best Soconusco chocolate, and they would find
themselves thanking God for their supraperfect digestive
systems.

"This gives me a chance here to put down an observation
the correctness of which may be counted on:

"When you have breakfasted well and fully, if you will
drink a big cup of chocolate at the end you will have
digested the whole perfectly three hours later, and you will
still be able to dine . . . Because of my scientific enthusiasm
and the sheer force of my eloquence I have persuaded a
number of ladies to try this, although they were convinced it
would kill them; they have always found themselves in fine

shape indeed, and have not forgotten to give the Professor his rightful due.

"People who habitually drink chocolate enjoy unvarying health, and are least attacked by a host of little illncsses which can destroy the true joy of living; their physical weight is almost stationary: these are two advantages which anyone can verify among his acquaintanceship and especially among his friends who follow this diet."

A floating tray of hot chocolate was part of the healthful morning ritual of a French dandy (left) in the early nineteenth century. More rugged souls took their cocoa mixed with health-giving Icelandic moss (below) later in the century.

Around the turn of the century cocoa was often advertised as the bringer of "health, strength and beauty" to the frail.

Beauty and Cocoa Butter

One of the main uses for cocoa butter, apart from its addition in the manufacturing of eating chocolate, is in the cosmetics industry. Its purity, its stability and the fact that it melts at skin temperatures makes it an ideal ingredient for oil based preparations.

Cocoa butter can, indeed, be classed among luxury beauty items. But rather than going out and spending money on some expensive, prettily packaged and heavily advertised commercial product, you can easily learn to prepare your own beauty aids with the help of pure cocoa butter, which is available in wrapped foil packages, like chocolate bars or butter, from most drugstores.

A very basic way to use your cocoa butter is as a sunbathing cream. Granted, it will not save you from sunburn. But then a surprisingly limited number of suntan potions can actually do that; it is up to you to guard against taking too much sun at one time. Where cocoa butter can help, however, is in preventing the dryness that results from exposure to the sun. Just take a small piece of cocoa butter and rub it on your skin; it should melt on contact, especially if the rubbing is taking place in the warm outdoors. (And by the way, be sure to keep the rest of your cocoa butter sheltered in a cool, shady place, or it will melt away.) You will notice a gentle aroma of chocolate, which should be an added advantage to you if you are sunbathing with a loved one who appreciates chocolate.

You will probably be inspired to experiment with cocoa butter in other beauty preparations. To start you off, here is a recipe for a simple facial mask.

Run a few inches of hot water into your bathroom sink, and set a small bowl in the water. Place in the bowl two tablespoons each of clear honey and finely ground oatmeal, and two teaspoons of cocoa butter. The warmth from the water will enable you to mix them together into a fine, smooth paste, which should take you a few minutes.

Now generously apply the mask all over your face, and leave it there for half an hour. Rinse it away with warm water, and gently pat your face dry. (You can also use the preparation to sooth and soften work-roughened hands.)

You will find that, with the aid of cocoa butter and other natural ingredients, you can actually make yourself feel more naturally beautiful and healthy.

Chocolate and Art

The manufacture of chocolate is often referred to as being an art; certainly more than just technological skill is responsible for the array of fine chocolate products that are produced throughout the world. It is no wonder, then, that chocolate has, in its own right, been the inspiration for and the subject of works of art.

Early works of art relating to chocolate were the illustrations accompanying accounts of the new food discovery from the new world. More than mere botanical drawings, these were often interpretative, heroic engravings that befitted chocolate's mythical origins. One Latin study from the early seventeenth century, for example, carried as its frontispiece a grand representation of Neptune, king of the seas, standing on his shell-decked chariot surrounded by his mermen minions, beneath a wind-whipped sky. A noble Indian maiden standing on the shore is handing to him a box bearing in inscription "INDA CHOCOLATA"—the chocolate that he will be entrusted to carry through his kingdom to the farthest of shores.

The morning bath for this German beauty was not complete without her billet-doux and a cup of chocolate.

The beginning of the eighteenth century saw still another form of chocolate-inspired art—the chocolate pot and chocolate service, known as *chocolatières* to the French, whose refined enjoyment of chocolate demanded such equipment. Some services were executed in the finest silver, but more and more the art of pottery took over. Soon chocolate pots appeared in such disparate styles as the symmetrical blue and white pendant patterns of Rouen, and the exquisitely delicate, pale Oriental flowers of the Strasbourg potteries.

Four examples of the treasures that can be collected by the chocolate connoisseur: an English silver chocolate pot crafted in 1777–78 (above); and two porcelain chocolate pots and a cup and saucer (right), all made in Holland in the eighteenth century.

The nineteenth century produced yet another chocolate art form—the chocolate box. This is reputed to have been invented in 1868 by Richard Cadbury, of the famous English firm, who thought that sentimental, colorful pictures of puppies or children might just sell more chocolate. He was right, and soon the chocolate box grew more elaborate, taking on all the lace, gilt and plush associated with Valentine art, as chocolate itself became more and more an offering of love.

The nineteenth century saw the development of lavish chocolate boxes, covered with materials such as velvet and brocade (above); adorned with sentimental pictures (below); shaped like hearts (left); and even decorated directly from nature (below left).

An Art Deco chocolate box, (above) is decorated with a scene of Egyptian inspiration. Other chocolate box innovations include a container in the shape of the chocolate tablets within (above right) and a box disguised as a guidebook (right) with a convenient fold-out map of Switzerland – the land of chocolate.

Cadbury's chocolate box might be considered an early form of popular art. Certainly the popular, or ''pop,'' arts of our modern times are at least partly a result of such commercial art. And because of that, chocolate itself has recently become the subject of the works of artists who may, to a greater or lesser degree, be considered serious. The colossal monuments and soft sculptures of Claes Oldenburg, for example, have included such items as gigantic models of

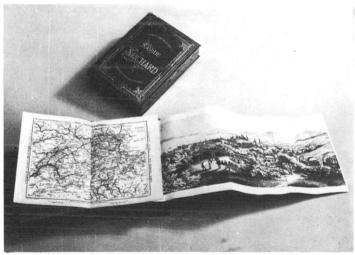

"Good Humor" bars—the popular American chocolate-covered ice cream bars. And many younger artists, taking a cue from Oldenburg and others, are creating art works inspired by the fine art of chocolate creation: wooden chocolate cakes, ceramic chocolate bars, sewn and stuffed soft chocolate creams and the like. Such works of visual wit can, in their own right, bring as much delight to the viewer as the real chocolate counterparts can to the eater.

Chocolat Sprüngli.

Schönwettermaschine im Jahre 2000.

Chocolat Sprüngli.

Bewegliche Häuser im Jahre 2000.

Chocolat Sprüngli.

Bewegliche Trottoire im Jahre 2000

Turn-of-the-century chocolate cards (above) gave people a taste of life in the year 2000, with weather machines, portable houses and moving sidewalks. A poster (above right) assured buyers of a product's goodness. Serious practicality is evident in a metal chocolate box (right) issued to British soldiers in the First World War.

van Houten's Cocoa

At Luncheon Van Houten's Cocoa is The Best.

One tea-spoonful is sufficient to make a delicious cup, sugar being added to taste. When ready, compare it with a cup of any other brand, and you will at once agree that for delicacy of flavor, and enticing aroma, Van Houten's is unequalled. By their special process of manufacture, the excess of fat is removed, and the resulting beverage made easily digestible, even by those who find ordinary cocoa apt to disagree with them. It makes a light, nourishing and delightful luncheon, and possesses the advantage of being at the same time the most economical in use.

Sold by all Grocers.   Don't forget to order it!

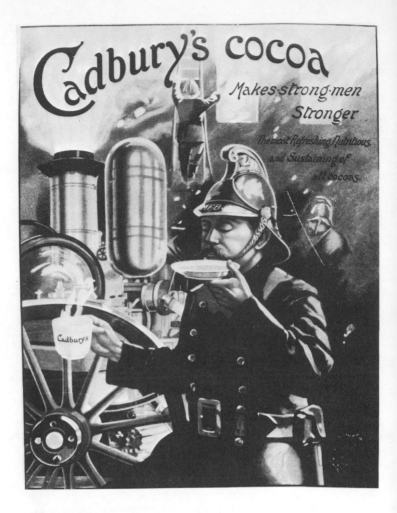

Collectors of chocolate ephemera can choose from posters (above), cutouts (below), containers (below right) or wrappers (above right).

CHOCOLAT SUCHARD

CHOCOLAT Ph. SUCHARD NEUCHATEL (SUISSE)

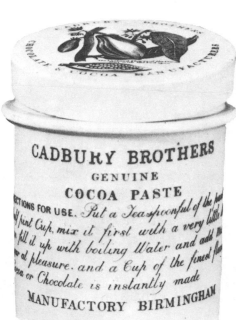

CADBURY BROTHERS
GENUINE
COCOA PASTE
DIRECTIONS FOR USE. *Put a Teaspoonful of the paste*
half pint Cup, mix it first with a very little
fill it up with boiling Water and add
at pleasure, and a Cup of the finest fla
Cocoa or Chocolate is instantly made
MANUFACTORY BIRMINGHAM

Duchamp's Chocolate Grinder

Virtually all of the pop artists acknowledge their greatest debt to the French pioneer of the Dada movement, Marcel Duchamp. And, surprisingly (although, perhaps, not . . .), one of Duchamp's key works—and a major figure in his greatest work, *The Bride Stripped Bare By Her Bachelors, Even*, also known as the *Large Glass*—was a painting of a French chocolate grinder, a small apparatus consisting of three grinding drums on a Louis XV base.

The depiction of the chocolate grinder, in two versions, enabled Duchamp to take a desired step away from the personal touch of the artist in art, to a more draughtsmanlike rendering of objects, as Calvin Tomkins relates in his excellent study of great avant-garde artists, *The Bride & the Bachelors*:

The Dada artist Marcel Duchamp made the chocolate grinder, a study of which is seen here, an important part of his greatest work.

"The first element of the *Large Glass* to take definite shape was the *Chocolate Grinder* of 1913, a precise rendering on canvas of the little machine that Duchamp had often seen in the window of a chocolate shop in Rouen. This painting, a study for the central organ of the "bachelor machine" in the *Glass*, was followed by another version in which the radial lines of the grinding drums, instead of being painted, were made by gluing and sewing white thread to the canvas—a mingling of paint and 'non-art' materials that had not as yet received the name of collage. Neither of these canvases look 'painted' in the usual sense, for the simple reason that Duchamp did not allow his hand to interfere with his mind. 'The problem was to draw and still avoid the old-fashioned form of drawing,' he has recalled. 'Could one do it without falling into that groove? Mechanical drawing was the answer—a straight line drawn with a ruler instead of the hand, a line directed by the impersonality of the ruler. The young man was revolting against the old-fashioned tools, trying to add something that was never thought of by the fathers. Probably very naïve on my part. I didn't get completely free of that prison of tradition, but I tried to, consciously. I unlearned to draw. The point was to forget *with my hand*.' "

In his notes on the *Large Glass* (translated, in the following quotes, by George H. Hamilton), Duchamp makes it clear what sort of role the chocolate grinder plays in the strange sexuality of his "bachelor apparatus":

"The *chocolate* of the rollers, *coming* from one knows not where, would deposit itself after grinding, as milk chocolate. . . ." And elsewhere, Duchamp points out that "The bachelor grinds his chocolate himself".

All that from a simple chocolate grinder! And more. An article entitled "The oscillating influence of Marcel Duchamp" (in the September 1973 issue of the journal *ARTnews*), by John Tancock of Sotheby Parke Bernet in New York, made the following claims for Duchamp's effect on his American contemporaries:

"Certainly the pair of works that exercised the most influence on American painters of this generation—John Covert, Charles Demuth, Charles Sheeler, and indirectly the whole of the Precisionist movement—were the two paintings of the *Chocolate Grinder*, both in the collection of Walter Arensberg by about 1918."

Poetry, Spirituality and Chocolate

The wholesome sweetness of chocolate has the power to inspire near-poetic praise from those who savor it. For some people, the love of chocolate can become an almost spiritual sensation.

Does this seem too high-flown a claim? Then have a look at this ode to chocolate:

> O tree, born in far off lands,
> Price of Mexico's shores,
> Rich with a heavenly nectar
> That will conquer all who taste it.
>
> To thee let every tree pay homage,
> And every flower bow its head in praise.
> The wreath of the laurel crowns you; the oak, the alder,
> And the precious cedar proclaim your triumph.
>
> Some say you lived in Eden with Adam
> And that he carried you with him when he fled.
> And from thence you journeyed to the Indes
> Where you prospered in the hospitable soil,
> And your trunk burgeoned with
> The bounty of your noble seeds.
>
> Are you another gift of Bacchus,
> Famed for his free-flowing wines?
> No—the fruits of Crete and Massica
> Bring not the glory you do to your native land.
>
> For you are a fresh shower that bedews the heart,
> The fountain of a poet's gentle spirit.
> O sweet liquor sent from the stars,
> Surely you must be the drink of the gods!

These five stanzas are a freehand translation from the original Latin (*"O nata terris Arbor in ultimis,/Et Mexicani gloria littoris . . ."*). They were written in 1664, not by some anonymous scribe but by a Jesuit priest, Aloysius Ferronius. That such poetic praise for chocolate should come from a man of the cloth is evidence enough of its ability to touch the spiritual side of man. Still greater support of this fact is that this ode to chocolate was dedicated to, and formed the basis for a work more generally praising Cardinal Francis Maria Brancaccio of the Vatican, who two years earlier passed the important judgment, *"Liquidum non frangit jenunum"*; liquids, amongst them chocolate, do not constitute a break of fasting.

Drama, Chocolate Creams and Romance

George Bernard Shaw billed his play *Arms and the Man*, first performed in 1894, as "An Anti-romantic Comedy." But romance there is in this delightful drama nonetheless—although of a clear-headed, non-starry-eyed sort. And it all hinges on a half-eaten box of chocolates and a man who comes to be known to us as the "Chocolate Cream Soldier."

The scene is the bedchamber of a young Bulgarian gentlewoman named Raina Petkoff. The year is 1885. Not far away, battle rages between the Bulgarians and the Servians. News has just come of a rousing Bulgarian victory, foolheartedly led by Raina's fiancé, Sergius, whose picture rests on top of her chest of drawers beside the aforementioned chocolate box.

Into Raina's bedchamber steals a Servian officer—in fact, a Swiss soldier of fortune—who has escaped from the battlefield. Bulgarian troops had pursued him through the streets. Raina, won over not merely by his plight but even more by his directness and his startlingly refreshing talk of the absurdity of war, conceals him from a search party. And she implores him to load his empty pistol to defend himself:

MAN. I've no ammunition. What use are cartridges in battle? I always carry chocolate instead; and I finished the last cake of that hours ago.

RAINA (*outraged in her most cherished ideals of manhood*) Chocolate! Do you stuff your pockets with sweets—like a schoolboy—even in the field?

MAN (*hungrily*) I wish I had some now.

Raina stares at him, unable to utter her feelings. Then she sails away scornfully to the chest of drawers, and returns with the box of confectionery in her hand.

A basket of cacao pods appeared in this work by Jacques Le Moyne, the first artist to visit North America, in 1564–65.

129

RAINA. Allow me. I am sorry I have eaten them all except these. (*She offers him the box*).

MAN (*ravenously*) You're an angel! (*He gobbles the comfits*). Creams! Delicious! (*He looks anxiously to see whether there are any more. There are none. He accepts the inevitable with pathetic goodhumor, and says, with grateful emotion*) Bless you, dear lady! You can always tell an old soldier by the inside of his holsters and cartridge boxes. The young ones carry pistols and cartridges; the old ones, grub. Thank you.

They later quarrel after he describes to Raina the quixotic actions of her fiancé on the battlefield. But, feeling true remorse and gratitude for what she has done for him, he says, "I know how good you've been to me: to my last hour I shall remember those three chocolate creams. It was unsoldierly; but it was angelic." And with great pity and compassion she says to him, "Come: don't be disheartened. Oh you are a very poor soldier—a chocolate cream soldier!" And Raina, and her sympathetic mother, Catherine, allow the exhausted Chocolate Cream Soldier to sleep the night away in the safety of Raina's room.

In the second act of Shaw's play, peace has been declared by treaty, and the Chocolate Cream Soldier returns. He is Captain Bluntschli, and, much to the chagrin of Raina and her mother, he has been befriended by both Raina's father and her fiancé. Raina first catches sight of him as Sergius is leading him into the house, and she quickly and skilfully covers up her momentary shock of recognition.

But with both men in her presence, Sergius appears more and more to Raina to be all huff and pretense, while the

Swiss/Servian captain speaks honestly from the heart. In the third act the story takes just about every twist that a romantic farce can take: the two men, both jealous suitors now, reach the brink of fighting a duel; a photo inscribed, "Raina, to her Chocolate Cream Soldier: a souvenir" and slipped by her into a greatcoat loaned to Bluntschli, slips in and out of old Petkoff's hands; the spurned Sergius is caught dallying with Raina's trusted maid and friend; and so on.

But in the end it becomes clear to all concerned that Raina is truly in love with Captain Bluntschli. He, in turn, manages to impress old Petkoff with a recounting of the material possessions he has acquired. Petkoff asks, *"with childish awe,"* if Bluntschli is in fact Emperor of Switzerland, to which the captain replies that he has the highest known Swiss rank: a free citizen. Raina, offered Bluntschli's hand, shows that she is not concerned with all these material possessions, but rather with the sensitive sensibility of the man who went to battle with cakes of chocolate in his holster:

RAINA (*pretending to sulk*) The lady says that he can keep his tablecloths and his omnibuses. I am not here to be sold to the highest bidder.

BLUNTSCHLI. I won't take that answer. I appealed to you as a fugitive, a beggar, and a starving man. You accepted me. You gave me your hand to kiss, your bed to sleep in, and your roof to shelter me—

RAINA (*interrupting him*) I did not give them to the Emperor of Switzerland.

BLUNTSCHLI. That's just what I say. (*He catches her hand quickly and looks her straight in the face as he adds, with confident mastery*) Now tell us who you did give them to.

RAINA (*succumbing with a shy smile*) To my chocolate cream soldier.

Chocolate and Love

Chocolate has been closely associated with love for hundreds of years. At first its sweet goodness caused people to think of it as something that released the innermost human passions—in a word, an aphrodisiac.

The Aztec emperor Montezuma, for instance, served ceremonial chocolate to nubile Indian maidens who were brought as offerings to him. Any awe-filled inhibitions they may have had are reputed to have been conquered by his special chocolate potion. Later, when chocolate came to Europe, certain self-righteous people looked askance at this drink that brought *so much* pleasure to those who consumed it. A religious essayist warned that it was responsible for the unholy lechery occurring among certain orders of monks. A writer in the British magazine the *Spectator*, on April 29, 1712, offered a caution to certain of his readers: "I shall also advise my fair readers to be in a particular manner careful how they meddle with romances, Chocolates, novels, and the like inflamers, which I look upon as very dangerous to be made use of. . . ."

But as chocolate gradually won widespread acceptance, the nature of its relationship with love changed. Where it had once been occasionally looked upon as a provoker of lustful love, it now became a sign of the purest affection, as exemplified by the sentimental chocolate boxes created by Richard Cadbury. A great deal of this change had to do, of course, with the continual improvements being made in the product, refining away any of the chocolate's rough, harsh qualities that might have been associated with the baser desires, and leaving a meltingly pure, smooth, wholesome and inoffensive product.

Today the superstitions that surrounded chocolate in the past seem very distant; and we have even outgrown some of that overblown nineteenth-century sentimentality. But chocolate must remain a food, and a gift, that will forever be associated with love—as long, at least, as we can also describe love with words that apply equally well to chocolate: "sweet" and "pure."

Chapter 5
Worldwide Chocolate Classics

Information

Recipes from Around the World

International Favorites

An Amazingly Versatile Food

Wherever you go in the world today, you are likely to find people enjoying chocolate. From the fast-and-ready food habits of Americans to the effortlessly perfect cuisine of the provincial French, it may be regarded as a favorite with everyone. Even the Japanese and other Asian nations to whom chocolate was, until fairly recently, a strangely foreign food are now importing cocoa and chocolate products in rapidly increasing quantities.

But beyond its consumption as a food in its simplest forms—the basic cocoa drink and a variety of chocolate bars—chocolate has great versatility. First, the cocoa drink itself varies amazingly from country to country, mixed to different strengths and sweetnesses with many different flavoring ingredients; some cocoa drinks actually reflect the historical development of chocolate, showing how that country changed the drink and how the drink itself changed when it passed beyond the country's borders. And, then, of course, chocolate and cocoa are used as ingredients in very many dishes throughout the world—including some main courses.

This chapter presents, alphabetically by country, some of the classic cocoa and chocolate recipes. Flip through them and you will be amazed by their exciting variety, and tempted, I hope, to try them all. (Before actually beginning a recipe, be sure to check over some of the general guidelines in the previous chapter on working with chocolate.) Do not, however, get overexcited and try to plan a whole meal around chocolate: it *is* possible, after all, to overdo a good thing.

AUSTRIA

Sachertorte

This is the famous cake created and sold at the Hotel Sacher in Vienna, which has the exclusive right, decreed in the highest Austrian court, to make and sell "genuine" Sachertorte.

But do not let law or fame intimidate you. Ersatz but still delicious Sachertortes are simple to make.

Bake two separate chocolate cakes according to the recipe on page 153. Spread the top of one with apricot jam, place the other on top, and coat the entire cake with the basic chocolate icing, a recipe for which appears on page 152. Serve with a helping of whipped cream.

BRAZIL

Brazilian Hot Chocolate

As should be expected, the chocolate flavor of the Brazilian drink is highlighted by a dash of two of the country's national drinks, coffee and rum. For one cup:

2 ounces (50 grams) plain chocolate	*dried orange peel*
	¾ cup milk
1 shot rum	*¼ cup strong black coffee*

In a saucepan, melt the chocolate with the rum. When melted, slowly stir in the milk and coffee. Beat until frothy, pour into a mug, add a twist of orange peel and serve.

ENGLAND

Cocoa Fool

There is nothing foolish about this traditional English dessert, here flavored with cocoa.

3½ cups (1 liter) double cream	½ cup cocoa
	½ cup sugar

Add the sugar to the cream and beat.

When the cream just barely begins to stiffen, gradually sprinkle in the cocoa while you continue beating. When stiff, chill before serving.

FRANCE

Chocolate Mousse

The best known French dessert, the most classic French chocolate recipe, and the most likely item to be served at the end of a trendy dinner party. There is no doubt that chocolate mousse is delicious and elegant; but you can make yours a mark above the average creation by adding a hint of orange flavoring with a splash of orange liqueur such as Cointreau or Grand Marnier.

To serve 4 to 6:

3 ounces (75 grams) semi-sweet chocolate	1 tablespoon orange liqueur
3 eggs, separated	

Melt the chocolate with the liqueur, and allow it to cool but still remain molten. Blend it with the egg yolks.

Beat the egg whites until they form very stiff peaks. Then fold them thoroughly into the orangey chocolate mixture.

Put the mousse into individual serving dishes, and chill thoroughly.

To vary the flavor of your chocolate mousse, try different liqueurs, or some strong coffee, in place of the Cointreau.

French Hot Chocolate

Instead of the morning *café au lait*, patrons of French cafés sometimes switch to a steaming cup of this strong, rich and not-too-sweet breakfast drink. For each cup you will need:

2 ounces (50 grams) semi-
   sweet chocolate
1 cup milk

1 egg yolk

Heat the milk, but do not boil. Pour all but a bit of it into a mug, and then add the chocolate to the remaining milk. Melt the chocolate over a low heat and blend thoroughly with the milk. Return the rest of the milk to the saucepan, remove from the heat, and stir.

Take a teaspoonful of the chocolate and milk mixture and stir it into the egg yolk. Add a few more teaspoons, and then pour the yolk mixture into the saucepan. Whisk the drink to a froth, and pour into the serving mug.

You might also like to try replacing half the milk with strong, hot black coffee, for a cup of hot mocha chocolate.

GERMANY

Steamed Chocolate Pudding

A rich and hearty dessert often served with the midday meal in Germany.

2 tablespoons butter,
   softened
4 ounces (100 grams)
   chocolate
¾ cup milk

¾ cup brown bread crumbs
¾ cup cake crumbs
¼ cup grated almonds
4 eggs, separated
¼ cup (50 grams) sugar

Butter a large steamed pudding mold with cover.

In a saucepan, melt the chocolate in the milk over a gentle heat. Mix all the crumbs and almonds together in a bowl, and pour the melted chocolate and milk over them. Mix well, and let it cool to room temperature.

Beat together the egg yolks and sugar until foamy. Add it to the cooled crumb mixture and mix well.

Beat the eggwhites until stiff. Fold them carefully into the pudding mixture. Pour into the mold and cover.

Steam until set—about 1½ hours. Turn out and serve with whipped cream.

GREECE

Chocolate-Nut Morsels

These tasty balls of candy are popular throughout Greece.

8 ounces (200 grams) plain chocolate
1 cup ground walnuts
½ cup chopped pistachio nuts
confectioner's sugar
1 teaspoon Greek brandy
1 teaspoon rosewater
1 teaspoon sugar
1 teaspoon cinnamon

Melt the chocolate over a gentle heat. Remove from the heat and stir in the nuts, brandy, rosewater and cinnamon. Form into bite-size balls and roll in confectioner's sugar.

HOLLAND

Cocoa Brittle

This delicious Dutch candy is traditionally formed in a large flat pan and is broken into pieces by hand. But you can also make it into circular morsels that are similar to pralines.

1 cup white sugar	*3 tablespoons cocoa*
1 cup brown sugar	*2 tablespoons butter*
½ cup single cream	*1 cup chopped roasted*
a pinch of salt	*walnuts or pecans*

Use 1 tablespoon of butter to grease a medium sized cake pan. Combine both sugars, the cream and the salt in a heavy saucepan over a medium heat. Stir continually, and when bubbles begin to appear, reduce the heat and add the cocoa and the remaining butter. Stir well until blended, then leave it to cook for about 10 minutes.

Test for consistency by dropping a bit into a cup of cold water; when it forms hard threads, it is ready. Remove from heat, stir in the nuts, and spread the mixture in the cake pan. Leave to cool to room temperature.

ISRAEL

Cocoa Cheesecake

Cheesecake is a classic Jewish dessert. Here it is given the added flavor of cocoa.

For its crust assemble:

1 cup biscuit or cookie crumbs	½ cup (100 grams) unsalted butter, softened
1 tablespoon sugar	

And for the filling:

1½ pounds (600 grams) cream cheese	1 teaspoon vanilla extract
1 cup sugar	4 eggs
2 tablespoons plain flour	¼ cup sour cream
	¼ cup cocoa

Preheat the oven to 300° F (150° C or Mark 2).

Knead together the crust ingredients until well mixed. Line a pie tin with the crust and chill in the refrigerator.

Beat the cheese until it is soft, then gradually mix in the sugar. Then, one after the other, stir in the flour, vanilla, eggs and sour cream. Finally, gradually blend in the cocoa.

When thoroughly mixed, pour into the chilled pie shell, and bake for an hour. Remove and cool to room temperature, then chill in the refrigerator before slicing and serving.

ITALY

Chocolate Torrone

This is the most exquisitely delicious of the nougats, or *torroni*, made in Italy. It is very simple to prepare; but beware of making it on your own: it must be one of the all-time great downfalls of compulsive tasters.

½ cup honey	1 cup cocoa
1 cup sugar	4 tablespoons water
2 egg whites, stiffly beaten	1 egg yolk
1 cup plain cookies or biscuits, broken into small pieces	1 cup mixed, roasted hazelnuts and almonds, finely ground

In a heavy saucepan heat the honey and sugar together, with a tablespoon or so of water, until they begin to caramelize. Remove from heat and slowly mix in the egg whites until smoothly blended.

In another pan, combine the cocoa with 3 tablespoons of water and stir over a low heat until smooth. Then mix it with the previous ingredients and stir in the egg yolk and the nuts. Blend well, and, finally, fold in the cookies or biscuits. Pour into a greased loaf pan, refrigerate for several hours, and then slice and serve.

JAMAICA

Chocolate Rum Liqueur

Most people are familiar with the chocolate flavored liqueur known as crême de cacao, which originated in the West Indies but has since achieved greater refinement in fashionable drawing rooms. You can stare the fashionable establishment right in the eye, singlemindedly going native with this recipe for your own chocolate liqueur.

8 ounces (200 grams) baking
   chocolate
4 cups (1 liter) Jamaican
   rum
1 vanilla bean

4 cups (1 liter) sugar syrup
8 cups (2 liters) water

Grate the chocolate and mix it with the rum. Add the vanilla. Allow it to steep for a week, then filter and add the syrup and the water. Mix well, and filter once more.

You can add this liqueur to your regular cup of hot chocolate for a really unusual kick. Or use it as a delicious topping for ice cream. Or, of course, you can enjoy it on its own or accompanying a cup of coffee.

MEXICO

Mexican Hot Chocolate

The drink as enjoyed today in the place where Europeans first discovered it almost half a millennium ago:

8 ounces (200 grams)
  unsweetened chocolate
3 tablespoons honey
1 teaspoon cinnamon

$\frac{1}{2}$ teaspoon nutmeg
1 cup water
3 cups milk

Melt the chocolate with the honey, the cinnamon and nutmeg, and the water, over a low heat. Stir until they are thoroughly blended, then add the milk and heat to boiling. Reduce the heat, and then beat it to a thick froth. Serves four to six.

More likely than not you will use an egg beater or a wire whisk to accomplish this last task. How much better, though, if you can find an ethnic import shop that can sell you a Mexican molinillo, *or chocolate mill, which is exquisitely carved and is simply twirled between your outstretched palms.*

Mole

Mole (pronounced to rhyme, more or less, with *olé*) is the star performer in Mexico's national dish—a rich and spicy sauce for turkey, chicken, pork or other meats. And its special ingredient is chocolate.

No certain explanation exists for the origin of *mole*, although the recipe has been known in various forms since the sixteenth century. However, there is a surprising similarity between the sauce's ingredients and those of Aztec chocolate, especially in the use of peppers and ground corn (the *mole*'s share coming from *tortillas*).

In its classic form, *mole* is made with turkey, as described below, and is called *mole de poblano de guajolote*. If you wish, it is easy to substitute equivalent quantities of other meats.

To serve eight hearty eaters you will need:

The meat:
1 large turkey, jointed and then cut into large serving pieces

a few tablespoons lard or cooking oil

boiling salted water to cover the turkey

The sauce:
8 green chili peppers, seeded
2 tablespoons toasted sesame seeds
1 cup roasted peanuts
2 fried tortillas
3 cloves garlic, finely chopped
1 medium onion, chopped
3 large tomatoes, chopped
½ cup raisins

thyme, marjoram and bay leaf
½ teaspoon cloves, ground
1 teaspoon cinnamon
1 teaspoon aniseed
½ cup lard or other cooking fat
pepper and salt
2 ounces (50 grams) unsweetened chocolate, grated

Brown the turkey pieces on all sides in the fat. Transfer them to a deep pot or casserole, cover with the boiling salted water, and simmer, covered, for about an hour.

For the mole *sauce, begin by frying the garlic and onions in a little bit of fat until they are transparent but not yet colored. Add the tomatoes and cook until the mixture thickens.*

Pulverize the chili peppers, sesame seeds, nuts and tortillas (it is most convenient to give them a whirl in an electric blender). Stir them into the mixture of tomatoes, garlic and onions, and add the raisins, herbs and spices. Melt the remainder of the cooking fat, and add all this mixture to it; stir at a high heat until well blended, then simmer. Season to taste with salt and pepper.

Finally, stir the mole into the turkey casserole, and simmer for another half hour. During the last few minutes, blend in the chocolate, which will enrich and unite the sauce into a surprisingly harmonious whole.

Gruesome skulls shaped from chocolate and decorated with icing teeth and eyes are sold during Mexican religious festivals.

SOVIET UNION

Brown Russian

A hot chocolate drink to keep you warm through the coldest
of Russian winters. For each cup:

2 ounces (50 grams) semi-   *1 shot vodka*
sweet chocolate   *1 cup milk*

*Heat the milk gently. Pour all but a bit of it into a mug. Add the
chocolate to the remaining milk, and melt over a low heat until
thoroughly blended. Return the rest of the milk to the pan,
remove from the heat and stir.*

*Pour the drink back into the mug. Stir in a shot of vodka and
serve.*

SWITZERLAND

Chocolate Fondue

It seems that whenever the cookery of Switzerland is
mentioned, fondue is what first comes to mind. This
chocolate fondue makes an ideal treat for a winter party.

1 pound (500 grams) semi-   *a splash of your favorite*
sweet chocolate   *liqueur*
½ cup whole milk

*Melt the chocolate and the milk together in a fondue pot or
saucepan over low heat until they have blended smoothly. Stir
in the liqueur, and keep the mixture warm for serving, either in
the fondue pot or in a chafing dish.*

The real enjoyment of a chocolate fondue comes in the variety of dipping materials, skewered on long forks and held in the molten mixture until fully coated. The most traditional item is squares of pound cake; other baked goods for dipping can include any sort of cookie or biscuit, or even pretzels. Fruits are even more delightful; try chunks of apple, slices of banana, dates, pitted cherries, pieces of pineapple, or anything else your imagination tells you might be tasty.

TURKEY

Sultan's Delight

Perfumed, rose-colored, gelatinous squares of Turkish Delight make an elegant accompaniment to coffee and aperitifs. Morsels of this popular candy are often covered in chocolate; but a simpler, and even more delicious, alternative is to make these rich brown, chocolate flavored confections, which are fit for a sultan's table. All you need are:

4½ tablespoons unflavored powdered gelatin
½ cup cocoa powder
⅓ cup powdered sugar
½ cup shelled, unsalted pistachio nuts

3 cups sugar
1½ teaspoons vanilla essence
⅓ cup shredded coconut
cold water
cornstarch

Add the gelatin to ¾ cup of cold water, and let it stand for fifteen minutes. In a saucepan, combine another cup of cold water with the cocoa and the three cups of sugar; stir over a medium heat until the sugar has dissolved. Then add the dissolved gelatin and bring to a boil.

Reduce the heat to a bare simmer, and leave it undisturbed for about twenty minutes. Then remove the saucepan from the stove, stir in the vanilla and the nuts, and let the mixture cool for half an hour or so.

Dust the bottom of a medium-size, shallow baking tray with cornstarch to prevent sticking, and pour in the delicious brown mixture. Give it a day to set; then cut it into one-inch squares and roll them in coconut and powdered sugar.

UNITED STATES

Chewy Chocolate Brownies

Chewy, fudge-rich brownies are a traditional American treat—the favorite snack in children's lunch boxes or special treat at the bottom of the family picnic basket. This recipe will make a generous three to four dozen brownie squares.

8 ounces (200 grams) baking chocolate	1 teaspoon vanilla
½ cup (100 grams) butter	1¼ cups (125 grams) flour, sifted
2 cups (350 grams) sugar	½ teaspoon salt
3 eggs	1 cup chopped nuts (optional)

Preheat your oven to 325° F (160° C or Mark 3).
Melt together the chocolate and butter, blending well. Remove

from the heat and stir in the sugar, then thoroughly blend in the eggs and the vanilla.

Add the flour, and the nuts if you want them, and quickly stir the mixture. Pour into a greased baking pan, and pop into the oven for about half an hour. Keep an eye on it though; if you overbake them they will dry out and will not be as chewy. Cool, and cut into squares or bars.

Chocolate Chip Cookies

These classic American cookies are best eaten with a glass of cold milk. They are supposed to cool after baking, but just try to keep them out of your mouth while they are still hot and chewy.

For about 3 dozen cookies:

6 ounces (150 grams) butter, softened	1 egg
¾ cup brown sugar	½ teaspoon baking soda
½ teaspoon salt	1½ cups plain flour
1 teaspoon vanilla extract	1 cup plain chocolate chips

Preheat the oven to 375° F (190° C or Mark 5).

Beat together the butter (all but a tablespoon), sugar, salt and vanilla until light and creamy. Blend in well the egg and baking soda, then gradually beat in the flour. Finally, fold in the chocolate chips.

With the remaining spoonful of butter, grease a baking sheet. Using a teaspoon, drop the batter onto the sheet, leaving enough space for the cookies to spread. Bake for 10 minutes or so, until their tops just begin to brown. Remove and cool on a wire rack (if you can wait).

INTERNATIONAL FAVORITES

Basic Chocolate Icing or Filling

A rich, all-purpose icing or filling for chocolate or other cakes.

4 ounces (100 grams)
  baking chocolate
1 tablespoon butter
1 cup double cream
1 cup sugar

1 egg, lightly beaten
a pinch of salt
1 teaspoon vanilla extract

Melt the chocolate, add the butter, cream and sugar. Simmer a few minutes, stirring with a wooden spoon, until the coating is of a consistency that forms a ball if a spoonful is dropped in cold water.

Add a few spoonfuls of the mixture to the egg, mix well and then quickly stir the egg into the saucepan. Add the salt and vanilla, and continue cooking and stirring until the icing coats the spoon well.

Cool to room temperature, then ice or fill the cake.

For variations, use different sorts of chocolate and, according to their sweetness, decrease slightly the amount of sugar. Try also substituting sour cream for half the cream, for a tangy frosting; or use strong coffee in place of the vanilla.

Basic Chocolate Sauce

This simple sauce can be poured over a wide range of desserts, chocolate or otherwise. Use your imagination.

You need equal volumes of:
sugar
water
cocoa

Boil the sugar and water together over a high heat for three minutes. Remove from the heat and quickly stir in the cocoa until well blended. Serve hot or cold.

For a richer sauce, substitute single cream for a quarter of the water, but stir it in after the cocoa has been added.

Chocolate Ice Cream

The best way to enjoy chocolate on a hot summer day. A touch of coffee in the ice cream highlights the chocolate flavour.

3½ cups (1 liter) double cream

4 ounces (100 grams) plain chocolate, broken into small pieces

1 teaspoon vanilla extract

1 teaspoon instant coffee

Gently heat the cream in a saucepan until it bubbles slightly. Remove from the heat, and add the chocolate, vanilla and coffee. Stir until the chocolate melts and blends completely. Cool to room temperature, then refrigerate.

When the mixture is cold, freeze in a home ice cream freezer. Or pour it into a large ice cube tray with the partitions removed and put in the freezer. When it begins to crystallize, beat well with a fork to break up the crystals. Return to the freezer, and when almost frozen solid beat again. Then cover with plastic wrap or foil and freeze before serving.

Rich Chocolate Cake

A simple recipe for a cake that tastes anything but simple.

4 ounces (100 grams) butter, softened

3 ounces (75 grams) sugar

1 teaspoon vanilla extract

6 eggs, separated

4 ounces (100 grams) plain chocolate

a pinch of salt

1 cup (100 grams) flour

Preheat the oven to 350° F (180° C or Mark 4). Use a teaspoon of butter to grease a cake tin.

Cream together the butter, sugar and vanilla. Melt the chocolate and blend it in. Then gradually beat in the egg yolks and salt.

Beat the egg whites until stiff. Slowly fold them in. Finally, gradually seive in the flour until completely mixed.

Pour the mixture into the tin and bake for about 45 minutes, until a toothpick inserted into the cake comes out clean. Then remove, and cool to room temperature. Fill or frost as you wish.

Illustration Acknowledgements

The Author and Publisher would like to thank the following for permission to use illustration material or extracts of original texts in this book:

Ardea 12. Bendicks (Mayfair) Ltd 86, 103. Bodleian Library, Oxford (Johnson Collection) 105, 108, 111, 131, 132. Boots Co Ltd 94, 95. British Museum of Natural History 39. Camera Press Ltd 36. Cadbury's Bournville 25, 28, 42, 43, 52, 53, 56, 58, 59, 69, 71, 99, 109, 119 top, 123 bottom, 124 top, 125 bottom. Chocolats Poulain 95. Chapman, Sue 91. Dickins, Douglas 20. Elite Chocolates, Tel Aviv 95. Floris Chocolates 94. Florence, Biblioteca Medicea Laurenziana 15. Gala Peter 34, 95. Gluck Press Archive 2, 23, 27, 33, 34, 44, 45, 66, 92, 97, Endpaper 2, 159. Hershey Food Corporation 31, 75. Lindt Sprüngli AG Endpaper 3, 35, 70–71, 80, 107, 122. Lockwood, Arthur 10, 54, 57 (ph. P B Redmayne), 62, 128. Mansell Collection 41, 46, 76, 78, 112, 123 top, 156. McGee, Shelagh 9, 24, 65, 87 bottom right, 88, 100, 101, 102, 130, 133, 134, 135, 136, 137, 138, 139, 140, 141 bottom, 142, 143, 144, 145, 146, 148, 150, 151, 152. New York Cocoa Exchange Inc 61, 63. Opie, Robert 104, 118 top, 119 bottom, 120. Ortiz, Marcos 147. Philadelphia Museum of Art 126. Radio Times Hulton Picture Library 13, 18, 21 top, 74, 80, 110, 114–115, 117. Reveille, photo Jack Curtis 84–85. Rowntree Mackintosh Ltd. 51 top, 89. De Ruijter b.v., Baarn 87. Staatliche Kunstsammlungen (Gemäldegalerie Alte Meister), Dresden 4. Suchard S.A. 32, 87 top, 118 bottom, 121, 125 top, Endpaper 158. Van Houten 29, 77. Verkade, Koninklijke Fabrieken 67, 82 top, 87 bottom left. Victoria and Albert Museum, London 116.

Text Acknowledgements

George Allen and Unwin Ltd. and Doubleday Inc. for permission to use an extract from *Charlie and the Chocolate Factory* by Roald Dahl. The Society of Authors, Bernard Shaw estate for permission to use an extract from *Arms and the Man* by George Bernard Shaw. Alfred A. Knopf Inc. for permission to use an extract from M. F. K. Fisher's translation of *The Physiology of Taste* by Brillat-Savarin. The Viking Press, Inc., for permission to use an extract from *The Bride & the Bachelors* by Calvin Tomkins.

Back endpaper: Old advertisements and collector's cards are but two types of the fascinating ephemera that appeal to the chocolate connoisseur.